DENMARK VESEY

DENMARK VESEY

❦

Lillie J. Edwards

Senior Consulting Editor
Nathan Irvin Huggins
Director
W.E.B. Du Bois Institute for Afro-American Research
Harvard University

CHELSEA HOUSE PUBLISHERS
New York   Philadelphia

Chelsea House Publishers
Editor-in-Chief Nancy Toff
Executive Editor Remmel T. Nunn
Managing Editor Karyn Gullen Browne
Copy Chief Juliann Barbato
Picture Editor Adrian G. Allen
Art Director Maria Epes
Manufacturing Manager Gerald Levine

Black Americans of Achievement
Senior Editor Richard Rennert

Staff for DENMARK VESEY
Copy Editor Philip Koslow
Editorial Assistant Leigh Hope Wood
Picture Researcher Wendy P. Wills
Assistant Art Director Loraine Machlin
Designer Ghila Krajzman
Production Manager Joseph Romano
Production Coordinator Marie Claire Cebrián
Cover Illustration Vilma Ortiz

3 5 7 9 8 6 4 2

Library of Congress Cataloging-in-Publication Data
Edwards, Lillie Johnson.
    Denmark Vesey / Lillie Johnson Edwards.
      p.   cm.—(Black Americans of achievement)
    Includes bibliographical references.
    Summary: A biography of the black freedom fighter whose planned
slave revolt in 1822, while never materializing, caused South Carolina to pass severe laws restricting the education, movement, and occupation of free blacks and slaves.
    ISBN 1-55546-614-1
       0-7910-0250-0 (pbk.)
    1. Vesey, Denmark, 1767 (ca.)–1822—Juvenile literature.
2. Slaves—South Carolina—Charleston—Biography—Juvenile literature.   3. Afro-Americans—South Carolina—Charleston—Biography—Juvenile Literature.   4. Charleston (S.C.)—History—Slave
Insurrection, 1822—Juvenile literature.   [1. Vesey, Denmark, 1767
(ca.)–1822.   2. Slaves.   3. Afro-Americans—Biography.
4. Charleston (S.C.)—History—Slave insurrection, 1822.]
I. Title.   II. Series.
F279.C49N42   1990
975.7'9150049607302—dc20   89-22336
[B]   CIP
[92]   AC

CONTENTS

BLACK AMERICANS OF ACHIEVEMENT

RALPH ABERNATHY
civil rights leader

MUHAMMAD ALI
heavyweight champion

RICHARD ALLEN
religious leader and social activist

LOUIS ARMSTRONG
musician

ARTHUR ASHE
tennis great

JOSEPHINE BAKER
entertainer

JAMES BALDWIN
author

BENJAMIN BANNEKER
scientist and mathematician

AMIRI BARAKA
poet and playwright

COUNT BASIE
bandleader and composer

ROMARE BEARDEN
artist

JAMES BECKWOURTH
frontiersman

MARY MCLEOD BETHUNE
educator

BLANCHE BRUCE
politician

RALPH BUNCHE
diplomat

GEORGE WASHINGTON CARVER
botanist

CHARLES CHESNUTT
author

BILL COSBY
entertainer

PAUL CUFFE
merchant and abolitionist

FATHER DIVINE
religious leader

FREDERICK DOUGLASS
abolitionist editor

CHARLES DREW
physician

W.E.B. DU BOIS
scholar and activist

PAUL LAURENCE DUNBAR
poet

KATHERINE DUNHAM
dancer and choreographer

MARIAN WRIGHT EDELMAN
civil rights leader and lawyer

DUKE ELLINGTON
bandleader and composer

RALPH ELLISON
author

JULIUS ERVING
basketball great

JAMES FARMER
civil rights leader

ELLA FITZGERALD
singer

MARCUS GARVEY
black-nationalist leader

DIZZY GILLESPIE
musician

PRINCE HALL
social reformer

W. C. HANDY
father of the blues

WILLIAM HASTIE
educator and politician

MATTHEW HENSON
explorer

CHESTER HIMES
author

BILLIE HOLIDAY
singer

JOHN HOPE
educator

LENA HORNE
entertainer

LANGSTON HUGHES
poet

ZORA NEALE HURSTON
author

JESSE JACKSON
civil rights leader and politician

JACK JOHNSON
heavyweight champion

JAMES WELDON JOHNSON
author

SCOTT JOPLIN
composer

BARBARA JORDAN
politician

MARTIN LUTHER KING, JR.
civil rights leader

ALAIN LOCKE
scholar and educator

JOE LOUIS
heavyweight champion

RONALD MCNAIR
astronaut

MALCOLM X
militant black leader

THURGOOD MARSHALL
Supreme Court justice

ELIJAH MUHAMMAD
religious leader

JESSE OWENS
champion athlete

CHARLIE PARKER
musician

GORDON PARKS
photographer

SIDNEY POITIER
actor

ADAM CLAYTON POWELL, JR.
political leader

LEONTYNE PRICE
opera singer

A. PHILIP RANDOLPH
labor leader

PAUL ROBESON
singer and actor

JACKIE ROBINSON
baseball great

BILL RUSSELL
basketball great

JOHN RUSSWURM
publisher

SOJOURNER TRUTH
antislavery activist

HARRIET TUBMAN
antislavery activist

NAT TURNER
slave revolt leader

DENMARK VESEY
slave revolt leader

MADAME C. J. WALKER
entrepreneur

BOOKER T. WASHINGTON
educator

HAROLD WASHINGTON
politician

WALTER WHITE
civil rights leader and author

RICHARD WRIGHT
author

ON ACHIEVEMENT

Coretta Scott King

BEFORE YOU BEGIN this book, I hope you will ask yourself what the word *excellence* means to you. I think that it's a question we should all ask and keep asking as we grow older and change. Because the truest answer to it should never change. When you think of excellence, perhaps you think of success at work; or of becoming wealthy; or meeting the right person, getting married, and having a good family life.

Those important goals are worth striving for, but there is a better way to look at excellence. As Martin Luther King, Jr., said in one of his last sermons, "I want you to be first in love. I want you to be first in moral excellence. I want you to be first in generosity. If you want to be important, wonderful. If you want to be great, wonderful. But recognize that he who is greatest among you shall be your servant."

My husband, Martin Luther King, Jr., knew that the true meaning of achievement is service. When I met him, in 1952, he was already ordained as a Baptist preacher and was working toward a doctoral degree at Boston University. I was studying at the New England Conservatory and dreamed of accomplishments in music. We married a year later, and after I graduated the following year we moved to Montgomery, Alabama. We didn't know it then, but our notions of achievement were about to undergo a dramatic change.

You may have read or heard about what happened next. What began with the boycott of a local bus line grew into a national movement, and by the time he was assassinated in 1968 my husband had fashioned a black movement powerful enough to shatter forever the practice of racial segregation. What you may not have read about is where he got his method for resisting injustice without compromising his religious beliefs.

He adopted the strategy of nonviolence from a man of a different race, who lived in a distant country, and even practiced a different religion. The man was Mahatma Gandhi, the great leader of India, who devoted his life to serving humanity in the spirit of love and nonviolence. It was in these principles that Martin discovered his method for social reform. More than anything else, those two principles were the key to his achievements.

This book is about black Americans who served society through the excellence of their achievements. It forms a part of the rich history of black men and women in America—a history of stunning accomplishments in every field of human endeavor, from literature and art to science, industry, education, diplomacy, athletics, jurisprudence, even polar exploration.

Not all of the people in this history had the same ideals, but I think you will find something that all of them have in common. Like Martin Luther King, Jr., they all decided to become "drum majors" and serve humanity. In that principle—whether it was expressed in books, inventions, or song—they found something outside themselves to use as a goal and a guide. Something that showed them a way to serve others, instead of living only for themselves.

Reading the stories of these courageous men and women not only helps us discover the principles that we will use to guide our own lives but also teaches us about our black heritage and about America itself. It is crucial for us to know the heroes and heroines of our history and to realize that the price we paid in our struggle for equality in America was dear. But we must also understand that we have gotten as far as we have partly because America's democratic system and ideals made it possible.

We are still struggling with racism and prejudice. But the great men and women in this series are a tribute to the spirit of our democratic ideals and the system in which they have flourished. And that makes their stories special and worth knowing. •◗»

DENMARK
VESEY

1

A TICKET
TO
FREEDOM

DENMARK VESEY STOOD in front of the cashier's window and stared at the lottery ticket in the palm of his hand. He was usually somber and serious, but on this chilly December morning in 1799 the sight of the ticket made him want to shout with joy. Biting his lip was all he could do to keep from bursting into an undignified grin.

The cashier, shouting at Vesey to hand over the ticket, startled him out of his reverie. Vesey ignored the man and took one final look at the slip of brown paper before placing it on the ledge under the barred window. The cashier picked up the ticket, read each digit aloud, and then held the paper next to the list of winning numbers. He moved his finger along each line of the list until he came across the matching numbers on Vesey's ticket and read them aloud. Then, without saying a word to Vesey, he walked to the far corner of the room and squatted in front of a small black safe. Vesey could not see him, but he could hear the clicking noises of the safe as the cashier dialed the combination. It seemed to take forever.

After winning a lottery in December 1799, Denmark Vesey collected $1,500 from a cashier on Bay Street (shown here in the mid-1800s) in Charleston, South Carolina. Vesey used a portion of the money to buy his freedom from slavery the following month.

11

A carpenter in the 1800s—a popular occupation for urban slaves and free blacks, especially because it gave them a bit of control over their daily schedule. Vesey was one of 11 carpenters in early 19th-century Charleston.

As Vesey waited, he became aware of the large leather bag of carpenter's tools that was slung over his shoulder. In his excitement, he had forgotten it was there. But now, with the delay, it began to feel heavy. With a sigh of impatience, he lifted the bag from his shoulder and carefully placed it on the floor.

Finally, the clicking noises stopped, and Vesey could hear the cashier mumbling to himself as he counted out the lottery winnings. Just a few minutes earlier, Vesey had walked into the cashier's office with the exuberance of a man whose dreams had come true. But his urge to smile began to wane as the cashier proceeded to count the money for a third time.

Just as Vesey emitted another heavy sigh, the safe door slammed shut. The cashier stood up from his crouch and, for the first time, looked directly into Vesey's eyes. Clearly, he did not like what he saw: a 32-year-old slave whose eyes failed to beam at his recent good fortune. Vesey returned the white man's stare with a look that burned with fierce pride.

The cashier squeezed the wad of money in his hand. To him, Vesey was an uppity slave who needed to learn how to act in front of a white man. He wanted to be the one to teach him, but Vesey's glare stopped him. It indicated to the cashier what most of the black as well as white residents of Charleston, South Carolina, already knew: Denmark Vesey was a proud man who deeply objected to slavery.

The cashier threw the money onto the counter and turned his back to the slave. Picking up the money, Vesey counted it aloud in half the time it had taken the cashier. Although the man's back was to Vesey, he could tell that the cashier felt humiliated. For the first time that morning, Vesey allowed himself a small smile of satisfaction.

Vesey bent down to reach into his bag of tools and pulled out some twine and a knife. As he opened

Blacks collecting money from a cashier. Many slaves, including Vesey, used the small allowance given to them by their owners to purchase lottery tickets in the hope that they would win enough money to buy their freedom.

the blade, the cashier turned with a start. Vesey's grin widened to a full smile as he cut off a 10-inch piece of twine, rolled the bills into a tight bundle, and wrapped the string around the money. He proceeded to stuff the money into a large pocket in his jacket. Then he picked up his tool bag, tossed it over his shoulder, and headed for the door. He let out a rich, hearty laugh as he left the building.

Vesey joined the busy Christmas crowd on East Bay Street. The sun felt warm, but because it was still early in the day, the wind carried a slight chill that was common to winter mornings in Charleston.

He put his hands in his jacket pockets to keep them warm. As he did so, his right hand found the wad of money he had placed in the pocket. It was time to forget about the cashier and think instead about the money. Fifteen hundred dollars! It was more money than he had ever seen.

Going in no particular direction, Vesey walked briskly along the crowded streets of Charleston. Unlike most blacks, he did not step out of the way to allow whites to pass. He often walked this way, in deliberate defiance of his slave status. But today his

actions were inadvertent, and he failed to notice the stares and shouts that his behavior elicited. Today he just wanted to think about his good fortune and the future that would come of it.

Fifteen hundred dollars was more than enough money for Vesey to purchase his freedom from his master, Captain Joseph Vesey. The thought exhilarated Denmark. The captain had a new home in Charleston and needed only a few domestic slaves to do the work—a cook, a butler, a housekeeper, a manservant, and a coach driver. This left Denmark

A view of Charleston harbor, which Captain Joseph Vesey first visited in 1770. He returned to the city regularly and by 1774 had entered into business arrangements that prompted him to settle there nine years later.

A typical scene on a slave ship during the voyage from Africa to the West Indies. Vesey worked for two years on slave ships belonging to his owner.

with very little to do around the Vesey household. Although Joseph Vesey received some income from Denmark's work as a carpenter—since 1783, he had been hiring himself out throughout Charleston—the captain also had to assume the responsibility of supervising Denmark's jobs, his salary, even his movements. Surely this was more trouble than it was worth, especially because Denmark worked not only in town but at logging sites 20 miles outside Charleston.

Freedom, it seemed, would be in Denmark Vesey's future. The notion seemed almost too good to be true. Yet the joy he felt at the thought of his freedom could not erase the fact that Joseph Vesey had been his master for 18 years. The memory of those years filled Denmark with anger. He remembered his chores as the captain's personal slave. He recalled the first time he accompanied the captain on a trip to buy slaves in Africa. He pictured the men, women, and children who were stuffed into the hold of the ship, where many of them died. Some wore looks of pride or fear or anger. Others showed no emotion at all— they simply willed themselves to die rather than endure the pain and humiliation of enslavement. Vesey remembered, too, how the captain got richer and richer from these trips—wealthy enough to move to Charleston and leave the slave-trading business.

When Captain Vesey settled in Charleston, Denmark's life changed somewhat. He became a carpen-

The cramped hold of a slave ship made the passage from Africa a living hell. It was not uncommon for a third of the slaves to perish during the voyage, with a number of them choosing to commit suicide.

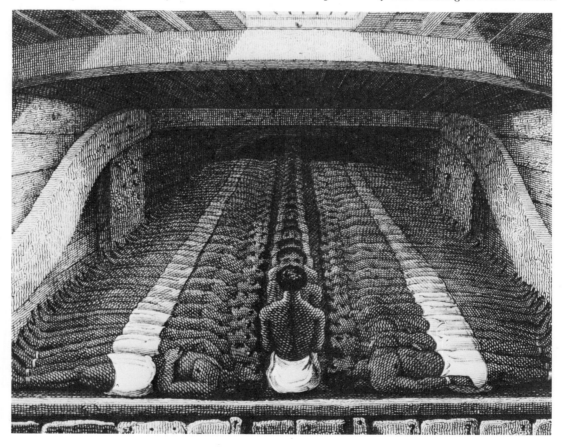

The U.S. Constitution permitted slave trading between Africa and America until 1808. This edict was not widely enforced, however, and slaves continued to be imported from Africa in the decades that followed.

ter, a common occupation for the few slaves who got the chance to learn a skilled trade. His work as a carpenter provided Vesey with more independence than he had ever known. But it did not give him his freedom. He was reminded of his bondage each time he handed over to the captain the money he made as a carpenter, as he was legally required to do.

The lottery winnings represented the very first time Denmark did not have to give money that had come into his possession to someone else. Fifteen hundred dollars! The money was his ticket to freedom.

As Vesey continued his walk, the church bell of St. Michael's sounded 12 o'clock. He had apparently been walking for hours and had missed his morning assignment. But it did not matter. He could easily finish the job in the afternoon and arrive home in plenty of time to talk to Captain Vesey before the day ended. Denmark had always possessed the ability to negotiate for his own freedom. And now that he had won the lottery, he had the means.

But Vesey would not stop at securing his own freedom. In the coming years, he would make use of all his resources and devise a plan to marshal thousands of slaves into an army. Together, he hoped, they would destroy Charleston and free all blacks in America from bondage. ☙

2

RITES OF
PASSAGE

DENMARK VESEY WAS born in 1767. It is
not known whether he was born in Africa or on the
island of St. Thomas in the Caribbean. In either case,
he was living on St. Thomas by the time he was 14
years old.

Like most Caribbean islands in the 18th century,
St. Thomas had an economy based primarily on sugarcane. Exporting this crop after it was refined into
cane syrup proved to be an extremely lucrative business for the white European plantation owners. By
taxing the landowners and merchants, the European
nations that claimed these islands as colonial pos-
sessions also benefited from the crop, as did the local
slave traders.

In fact, the slave trade in the Caribbean was especially profitable, because sugarcane, like tobacco
in Virginia and rice in South Carolina, was a labor-
intensive crop: Large numbers of workers were required to plant, cultivate, and harvest the cane and
refine it into sugar. Laborers stripped the cane stalks
of their leaves and then crushed the stalks for their
juice. This liquid was subsequently placed over a fire
in a huge vat. The heat concentrated the juice and
turned it into a thick, sugary syrup.

Slaves boiling cane syrup on a Ca-
ribbean sugarcane plantation. Be-
cause the process of harvesting
and refining sugarcane into cane
syrup demanded a large number
of laborers, Caribbean planters
required a steady supply of slaves
from traders such as Captain
Joseph Vesey, Denmark's owner.

Because of the tropical climate, sugar could be processed year-round. Thus, slaves on sugarcane plantations worked from before sunup to after sundown, day after day and year after year, performing the same tasks every season. For this physically demanding work, plantation owners preferred to purchase young slaves—many of whom wound up dying from either malnutrition or overexertion. The high death rate and low birthrate (because the planters imported twice as many men as women) meant that the slave population of the Caribbean had to be re-

plenished with shipload after shipload of new male slaves from Africa. And this meant big business for slave traders such as Joseph Vesey.

Vesey came from Bermuda, an island renowned for its expert shipbuilders and navigators, which made a career as a ship captain an easy choice for him. He owned at least five ships and traded lumber, rum, gin, molasses, sugar, meat, and other food products in the colonial port cities of South Carolina, Virginia, and New York; on the Caribbean islands of St. Thomas, St. Domingue, St. Croix, St. Kitts, Jamaica, Mar-

Slaves working on a Caribbean plantation—a fate that Vesey narrowly escaped because he was diagnosed as having epilepsy and therefore could not be sold legally to another slave owner. Instead, he served as Captain Joseph Vesey's personal slave.

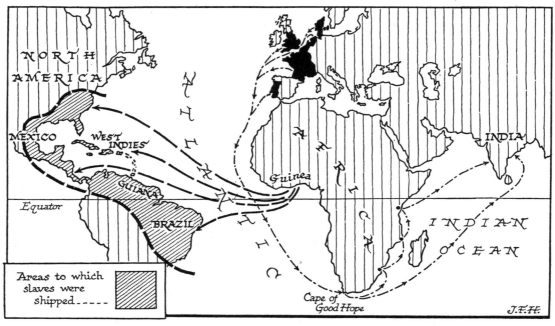

A map showing the principal trade routes that slave ships followed between Africa and the Americas. From 1781 to 1783, the years that Vesey sailed on slave ships, his owner concentrated on the route between Africa and the West Indies and avoided the revolutionary war in the North American colonies.

tinique, Barbados, and Bermuda; and along the coast of West Africa, in countries now known as Ghana, Togo, Benin, Nigeria, Cameroon, and Angola. And everywhere he traded goods, he also traded slaves.

In the 1770s, when the revolutionary war disrupted all trade with the British colonies in North America, Captain Vesey was forced to limit his dealings to Africa and the Caribbean islands. Even without the North American ports, his mercantile activities continued to bring in large profits because slaves were in great demand in the Caribbean. On St. Domingue, for example, French colonialists annually imported as many as 20,000 slaves to work on the sugar plantations.

In 1781, Vesey transported 390 slaves to St. Domingue. Among his cargo was a 14-year-old male who had been living on St. Thomas. Because the demand for male slaves was great, Vesey managed to sell the teenager to a French planter for what the captain considered a high price.

The deal soon turned sour, however. Three months later, the youth became seriously ill, prompting the irate planter to demand that Vesey refund his money. When a physician verified the planter's claim that the boy was not in perfectly good health—he was epileptic—Captain Vesey was compelled by law to buy back the slave. Accordingly, the captain repurchased the teenager and decided to keep him as his own property. Vesey named his new slave Denmark because the boy had been part of the shipment from the Danish colony of St. Thomas.

Denmark immediately became the captain's personal slave and began sailing with him throughout the Caribbean and along the African coast. From 1781 to 1783, Denmark saw all the activities of the slave-trading world. Whenever the captain lowered the sails and dropped anchor off the white sandy beaches of West Africa, Denmark was standing at his side, ready to help the captain change from the clothes he had worn during the journey to attire that was more suitable for negotiating with a slave trader on the coast. Then the two of them would wait for the slaver to send a canoe to bring Captain Vesey ashore.

As the warm waters of the Atlantic glistened under the hot rays of the morning sun, Denmark spent little time studying the beauty of the West African coastline. He could not stop himself from staring at a large thatched enclosure on the beach. It was a makeshift stockade filled with Africans. Some were bound by ropes, others by chains. Along with the young men who had their feet and hands locked in heavy shackles were women, some of them nursing babies, and children with tear-stained cheeks.

Joseph Vesey paid little attention to the miserable scene. An experienced slave trader, he looked to see which slaves were too old or too ill to command a good price at the slave markets on St. Domingue and

St. Thomas. To the captain, Africa was simply another place of business. Wherever he went ashore,
each man, woman, and child stood before him to be
examined like a horse, a house, or any other piece
of property that could be bought and sold. The captain checked their eyes, looked closely at their tongue
and teeth, peered down their throat, bent their arms,
checked their joints, and pinched their skin.

Denmark was forced to watch as human beings
became nothing more than cargo. Before his very
eyes, people were bartered in exchange for rum, gin,
molasses, sugar, cloth, guns, pistols, iron and lead
bars, shells, glass beads, salt, knives, fishhooks, to-

*A slave trader brings captured
Africans to the coast for sale.
Ironically, some African kingdoms
came to depend on the slave trade
as a major source of income.
Men, women, and children captured in tribal warfare were sold
into bondage.*

bacco, paper, copper, brass pans, cutlasses, silver, gunpowder, pots, kettles, and needles.

The captain's new slaves were brought from the beach to the ship by canoes. Once they were on board the huge vessel, Denmark pulled the door to the hold open to allow the crew to take the slaves below deck. The captain's men crammed the slaves side by side, body against body, and chained them onto small platforms. The slaves remained chained in this way for most of the journey across the Atlantic, which was known as the Middle Passage.

During the journey from Africa, the smell of human waste, disease, and death often overwhelmed Denmark. Chained below deck, spending day after day and night after night in the dank, dark hold, many slaves became ill and died. Others committed

A prospective buyer inspects a slave prior to a sale. Men, women, and children were exchanged not only for money but rum, sugar, or guns—whatever the seller needed most.

A slave is lowered into the hold of a ship—one of the many tasks that Vesey was forced to perform while sailing with his owner.

suicide by refusing to eat or by jumping overboard when they were taken above deck. And some fell into such despair that they seemingly willed themselves to die. A quarter to a third of the slaves that were shipped from Africa died along the way.

On occasion, crew members would scrub the hold with vinegar in an attempt to disinfect the slave quarters and prevent disease. During these times, the slaves were brought on deck. Under close guard, they were allowed to shuffle around the ship for a bit of exercise.

For two years, Denmark gazed into the eyes of these shackled prisoners and saw his own accursed fate staring back at him. He knew what it was like to exist only to serve others. By the time he was 16 years old, he had learned all about the slave trade:

the brutal treatment of the Africans and the profits that the sea captains and traders made. He had also discovered that any attempt to rebel was met with torturous punishment—whips, branding irons, and thumbscrews.

Just as branding irons were used to sear the flesh of the African captives, two years on a slave ship apparently burned the agony of the slave trade into Denmark's memory. When he looked in a mirror, he saw in his eyes the same anger, humiliation, and sadness that he had seen in the eyes of the slaves on the West African coast, on board Captain Vesey's ship, and on the auction block. Yet Denmark, despite all the cruelty he witnessed, learned to show none of his sadness and anger. Though his heart might burn with emotion, he revealed to the world only a solemn and steady gaze. ❦

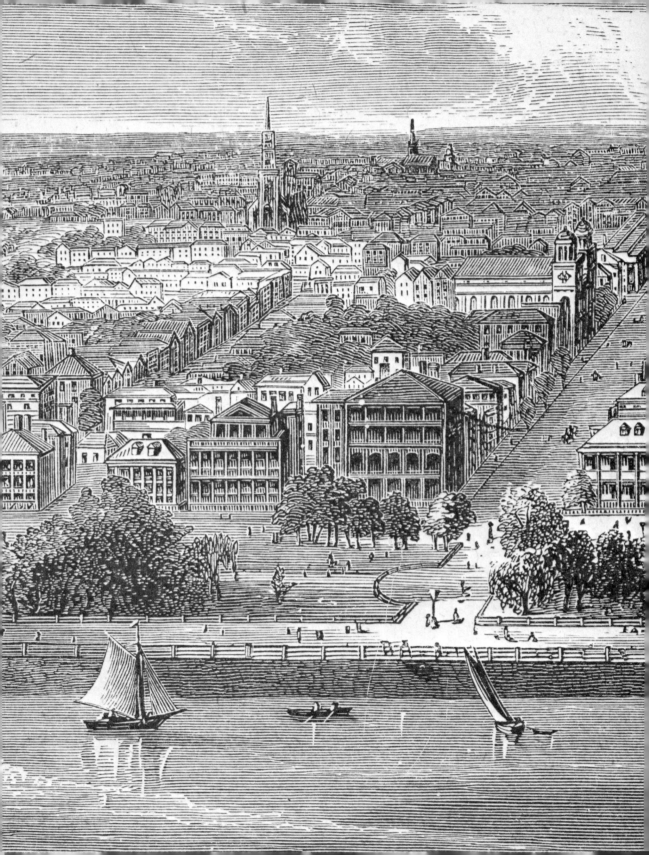

3

CAPTAIN
VESEY'S
SLAVE

UNLIKE THE SLAVES who lived in relative isolation on plantations and farms, Denmark Vesey became a very worldly young man as he sailed the Atlantic with Captain Vesey from 1781 to 1783. During those years, Denmark saw more of the world than most whites, and he carefully observed all the activities around him. While picking up the languages he heard—English, French, Danish, and Spanish—he also learned all he ever needed to know about slavery and slave trading in North America and the Caribbean.

Then, in 1783, Denmark found himself settling into the urban life of Charleston, South Carolina, chiefly because the market for slaves in America had begun to decline. Farmers in the North had started cultivating a variety of crops that required less intensive labor than was previously needed. They had found that hiring a poor European immigrant to work the land was far less expensive than paying for the permanent care of a slave.

In 1783, Captain Joseph Vesey gave up the slave trade and settled in Charleston, South Carolina. The city, which was then the fourth largest in America, boasted a busy harbor at the confluence of the Ashley and Cooper rivers and was an ideal place for the captain to establish a business dealing in ship's supplies.

In addition to abandoning slavery for economic reasons, many citizens of the new nation responded to their recent revolution by reassessing the moral, ethical, and political ramifications of slavery. The language of the Declaration of Independence seemed to prick the conscience of the American people. If "all men are created equal" and "are endowed by their Creator with certain unalienable rights," as the Declaration stated, then slavery had to be morally wrong and inconsistent with the high ideals of a democratic republic.

Indeed, many northern states had already begun drafting legislation to abolish slavery. In 1780, the newly adopted state constitution of Massachusetts prohibited slavery. Pennsylvania enacted laws to gradually end slavery. In time, New Jersey, New York, Connecticut, and other northern states followed Pennsylvania's example.

Although some southerners decided to free their slaves after the Revolution, the southern states still had economic incentives to keep slavery alive. In the late 1700s, the South's economy developed differently than that of the North. The South relied on cash crops—cotton, sugar, tobacco, indigo, and rice—that required intensive labor and were most profitable when grown in vast quantities. As a result, large plantations became common in the South, and their success depended largely on slave labor.

Nevertheless, many southerners were also interested in slowing down the slave trade. Their reason for doing so, however, was decidedly different from that of their northern neighbors: They feared the steady rise of the black population. From 1750 to 1790, Virginia's black population increased from 101,452 to 305,493; Maryland's, from 43,450 to 121,079; North Carolina's, from 19,800 to 105,824; Georgia's, from 1,000 to 29,662; and South Carolina's, from 39,000 to 108,895.

A copy of the first draft of the Declaration of Independence, which contained language strongly condemning slavery. These words were ultimately omitted from the final version of the document.

South Carolina, which boasted a black population of 44 percent shortly after the Revolution, tried to inhibit the slave trade in several ways. First, the state placed heavy duties on slave imports in 1783. But when that did not work, it prohibited all traffic in slaves, beginning in 1787. The suspension of the slave trade proved to be temporary, however. In 1803, a cotton boom made it a worthwhile gamble to own slaves once more.

As the slave trade declined in the United States after the Revolution, the constant demand by Caribbean sugar plantations for low-cost labor made for a thriving interisland slave trade. Instead of limiting

Slaves loading a boat with rice, one of the principal cash crops harvested on South Carolina plantations. A large portion of the crops that South Carolina exported to other states passed through Charleston by boat.

his trading to the islands and awaiting a change in the American market, Captain Vesey realized that profits lay not in the Middle Passage but in the urban centers of America. Accordingly, he settled in Charleston in 1783, one year after the last British troops left the city.

During the revolutionary war, plantation production had been brought to a standstill, property had

been destroyed, and the American currency had become worthless. And now that the war had ended,
Charleston was undergoing the difficult process of
renewal. Even though a great deal of labor was needed
to help rebuild the city, which was then the fourth
largest in America, and the surrounding plantation
economy, there was insufficient capital to invest in
slaves, building materials, and household goods.

Yet Charleston remained an important commercial and social center despite the economic stagnation caused by the war. More than 100 ships competed daily for docking space at its busy harbor, which was located at the confluence of the Ashley and Cooper rivers, just five miles from the Atlantic Ocean. Small boats brought produce from the local plantations to Charleston harbor, where ships from other states and other countries also docked. These larger vessels carried rum, sugar, and molasses from the Caribbean and manufactured goods such as furniture, clocks, and fabric from Europe. Slave ships came to the port, too. Slaves were auctioned there twice a week, as traders found buyers in spite of the newly imposed tariffs.

With its busy harbor, Charleston was an ideal place for Joseph Vesey to establish a new business. The city's war-ravaged economy offered vast opportunities for anyone who had capital to invest, and Vesey, having spent most of the war in profitable trade between the Caribbean islands and Africa, was ready to do so. He moved to King Street and began selling his cargo ships and slaves and investing in ships' supplies. In this way, he proceeded to relinquish his role in the slave trade and launch his career as a ship's chandler dealing in specialized goods.

When Denmark Vesey joined the captain in Charleston, he soon discovered that the local society was highly stratified along the lines of race, class, and gender. A few privileged, wealthy planter families formed a powerful ruling elite that controlled Charleston's political, economic, and social life. They owned most of the best land and the majority of the slaves in the area.

Charleston's elite lived in Georgian-style mansions built of stone and brick. Modeled after the homes of London's successful merchant class, these structures replaced those that were destroyed during the war. The new houses stood on narrow, unpaved

streets and featured covered passageways, called piaz-
zas, that led to ornate doorways. Behind each of these
mansions, a separate two-story building housed on its
ground floor the kitchen, stables, and storerooms.
Slaves—coachmen, grooms, footmen, butlers,
housekeepers, maids, and cooks—lived on the second
floor, in small, sparsely furnished rooms.

In Charleston, slaves were not only domestics for
the town's elite. They also worked for those on the
second tier of the social scale: railroad men, shipbuilders, merchants, lawyers, doctors, engineers, and
businessmen like Captain Vesey. In fact, slaves were
so numerous in Charleston that people who did not
own a slave could hire one for $6 to $10 a month.
Charleston's two rice mills contracted annually with
slave owners to hire out slaves. The city employed
slaves as firemen and as laborers for public services

*Produce and other goods are
brought from an outlying plantation to an urban market. Selling
these items at the market was a
common occupation for slaves in
Charleston.*

and public-works projects: building bridges, roads, canals, and sewage systems; cleaning the streets; and collecting garbage.

Slaves were also seen in Charleston peddling goods. They monopolized the city's three markets, selling fish (fishing was principally a slave occupation) at one market and produce from the local farms and plantations at the other two. In doing so, they worked under specific regulations. Before slaves headed off to sell their wares, their owners gave them tickets indicating the amount of fish or produce that the slaves had in their possession. Any attempt by slaves to sell unticketed goods for their own profit was punished. Moreover, slaves licensed as fishermen had to

Strict codes regulated the conduct of slaves within the market system. Any slave caught selling goods for his or her own profit was swiftly punished.

register with the city clerk; otherwise, they would be punished with 39 lashes and cancellation of their license.

Enjoying a variety of occupations, having access to better housing and food, and being exposed to a more cosmopolitan environment than their rural counterparts gave urban slaves a unique character. Rural slaves, by contrast, seldom left the confines of the plantation. They often spent months, years, even an entire lifetime within the plantation's boundaries.

Thus, when Captain Vesey became a city merchant, 16-year-old Denmark saw his life change as well. In addition to four free blacks, an East Indian woman, and a teenage apprentice, Denmark was one of eight slaves to reside in Joseph Vesey's household in Charleston. The slaves performed domestic tasks—they were the captain's cook, maid, and valet—and worked at semiskilled jobs: gardener, carriage driver, handyman. They also worked for Vesey's merchandising business: making deliveries, hauling packages, and even serving as clerks.

The free blacks in Vesey's household performed the same type of work but on a contractual basis. In a busy commercial center such as Charleston, it was especially economical to hire free blacks to help out periodically in one's household or business. They were always on hand to be hired when needed, and their wages were much lower than those paid to white laborers.

In several ways, urban slaves, especially skilled slaves, were like free blacks. They worked in a variety of occupations: They served as domestics, cooks in hotels and restaurants, washerwomen, nurses and midwives, sailors, fishermen, bricklayers, salesmen and clerks, seamstresses, porters, and blacksmiths. During periods when they were not needed by their owners, skilled slaves hired themselves out to other employers to do temporary work. The wages they earned went to their owners, and in turn the slaves received a small allowance to cover the cost of their food and clothing. Some slaves used part of this money to buy lottery tickets, while others saved what they could in the hope of purchasing their freedom.

Some slaves were even allowed to "live out"—establish an independent household. In Charleston, an entire community of "live-out" slaves and free blacks lived in the Neck, a neighborhood outside the city limits.

As a skilled carpenter, Denmark lived on the edge of the slavery system. Although Captain Vesey owned him and claimed his salary, Denmark commanded much of his own time and received a portion of his wages as an allowance. On the high seas, he had been an indispensable asset to the slave-ship captain, but in Charleston, Joseph Vesey had little need and even less time to supervise Denmark's activities. Moreover, Denmark was in no need of supervision. The intelligent and resourceful young man took advantage of the few opportunities available to a slave who was literate and worldly.

Urban life provided Denmark with opportunities he would not have had on an isolated plantation or rural farm. In Charleston, he had access to newspapers and read about current issues in the city and elsewhere. On street corners and in stores he was exposed to people who enjoyed exchanging opinions and arguing the issues of the day. He also held discussions with other slaves and free blacks who read the papers as avidly as he did. Captain Vesey's decision to settle in Charleston proved to be a fortuitous one for Denmark. ❧

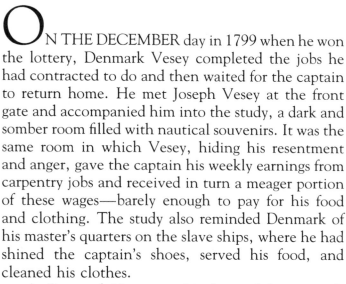

O N THE DECEMBER day in 1799 when he won the lottery, Denmark Vesey completed the jobs he had contracted to do and then waited for the captain to return home. He met Joseph Vesey at the front gate and accompanied him into the study, a dark and somber room filled with nautical souvenirs. It was the same room in which Vesey, hiding his resentment and anger, gave the captain his weekly earnings from carpentry jobs and received in turn a meager portion of these wages—barely enough to pay for his food and clothing. The study also reminded Denmark of his master's quarters on the slave ships, where he had shined the captain's shoes, served his food, and cleaned his clothes.

As Denmark Vesey stood in front of the captain's desk, his body leaned forward slightly, as if he were still on one of his master's ships in heavy seas. Without hesitating, Denmark asked to buy his freedom, informing the captain that the cash for the purchase was readily available. The captain did not pause at the news. He simply set a price of $600 and scheduled the sale to take place the following month.

In the 1800s, free blacks formed numerous organizations in an attempt to protect their rights and improve their lot. No group proved to be more influential than the black church, which sometimes convened secretly because laws passed by whites restricted black worship practices.

So, in January 1800, Denmark Vesey met once again with Joseph Vesey in the library. On a quiet winter evening, the slave gave his owner $600, and the captain in turn gave Vesey his manumission papers. After being the captain's slave for 19 years, Denmark Vesey was now a free man.

By paying $600 to Joseph Vesey, Denmark Vesey joined the small community of free blacks that lived in Charleston. There were slightly more than 1,000 of them, and they pursued a variety of occupations. There were seamstresses and tailors, hairdressers and barbers, cooks, blacksmiths, shoemakers, storekeepers, bricklayers, painters, contractors, merchants, coal and wood dealers, and fishermen.

But no matter how successful or hardworking free blacks might be, their freedom was as precarious as it was limited, for they mocked the slave system by their very existence. Whenever slave owners decided that one of their slaves deserved freedom, he or she was manumitted. In the eyes of such owners, the freeing of just one slave did not pose a threat to the system; the bestowal of freedom was simply an exception to the rule that all blacks should be slaves. Yet the existence of free blacks indicated that the system of slavery was imperfect, which indeed it was.

Blinded by the assumption that all blacks deserved, even needed, enslavement, the white community lived in a world of contradictions. On the one hand, they thought of free blacks as lazy and ignorant, incapable of working a steady job without being forced to do so. On the other hand, whites employed them in such highly skilled jobs as carpentry and were afraid that free blacks would become the shrewd leaders of slave rebellions.

To combat the contradictory feelings they entertained about free blacks, whites invented strategies to limit the size of the free black community and restrict the rights of its members. This was accomplished largely by implementing strict laws concerning the manumission of slaves. In South Carolina, it became increasingly difficult for slave owners to manumit their slaves. Denmark Vesey, for one, was especially lucky to have received his freedom in 1800. After the turn of the century, slaves and slave owners were questioned by a committee composed of five prominent citizens who judged manumission petitions. Eventually, South Carolina passed laws prohibiting the immigration of free blacks into the state and requiring written permission from the state legislature for manumissions.

As Vesey quickly learned, the slaves who received manumission papers never achieved total freedom. Free blacks had no way of protecting themselves from the hostility of whites—unlike slaves, ironically enough, who were deemed to be property and were protected by their owners. The South had decided

By Jacob Radcliff Mayor, and Richard Riker Recorder, of the City of New-York,

It is hereby Certified, That pursuant to the statute in such case made and provided, we have this day examined *one* certain *slave* Negro Slave named *George* the property of *John Delany*

which slave *is* about to be manumitted, and *he* appearing to us to be under forty-five years of age, and of sufficient ability to provide *for himself* we have granted this Certificate, this *twenty five* day of *April* in the year of our Lord, one thousand eight hundred and *fourteen*

Jacob Radcliff

R Riker

Register's Office Lib no 2 of Manumissions page 62 —
Mr S Slocum Register

As a free black, Vesey had to carry his manumission papers (which were much like the document shown here) at all times. Even though these papers proved his status as a free man, they failed to provide him with any legal guarantee that he would not be abducted and sold back into slavery.

that enslavement, rather than freedom, was the norm for blacks, and it established all sorts of barriers to limit black freedom.

Some of these barriers came into play every day. Vesey, like all free blacks, had to carry his manumission papers on his person at all times to prove his free status. He also needed to present them to pass the registration requirements for living in South Carolina. In addition, he had to pay two annual taxes: one, which amounted to $10, because he was self-employed in a trade; the other, a $2 poll tax required for residency. If he neglected to pay the latter tax, a sheriff could arrest him and sell his services to the highest bidder for a specified period of time (up to five years).

Vesey's freedom was threatened in other ways as well. Even if he followed the letter of the law, he still ran the risk of being kidnapped and sold again into slavery. Until 1837, there were no laws against abducting free blacks and selling them.

Indeed, the courts did little to protect the rights of free blacks. When accused of a crime, they were tried in the same way as slaves—without any legal representation. They were not judged by a jury of their peers but by a judicial committee made up of two justices of the peace and several landowners. A simple majority vote of the committee members was sufficient for conviction. No appeal of their decision was allowed.

Moreover, blacks were not permitted to serve on juries. Nor could a black, slave or free, testify against a white, no matter what the crime, no matter how strong the testimony and the evidence. Blacks were permitted, however, to testify against other blacks.

In the face of such overwhelming inequities, free blacks in Charleston united to help and protect each other. Like other free blacks in cities throughout the nation, they founded organizations to provide insur-

City of New-York, *ss.*

A LAW

For Regulating Negroes and Slaves in the Night Time.

BE It Ordained *by the Mayor, Recorder, Aldermen and Assistants of the City of* New-York, *convened in Common-Council, and it is hereby Ordained by the Authority of the same,* That from hence-forth no Negro, Mulatto or Indian Slave, above the Age of Fourteen Years, do presume to be or appear in any of the Streets of this City, on the South-side of the Fresh-Water, in the Night time, above an hour after Sun-set; And that if any such Negro, Mulatto or Indian Slave or Slaves, as aforesaid, shall be found in any of the Streets of this City, or in any other Place, on the South side of the Fresh-Water, in the Night-time, above one hour after Sun-set, without a Lanthorn and lighted Candle in it, so as the light thereof may be plainly seen (and not in company with his, her or their Master or Mistress, or some White Person or White Servant belonging to the Family whose Slave he or she is, or in whose Service he or she then are) That then and in such care it shall and may be lawful for any of his Majesty's Subjects within the said City to apprehend such Slave or Slaves, not having such Lanthorn and Candle, and forth-with carry him, her or them before the Mayor or Recorder, or any one of the Aldermen of the said City (if at a seasonable hour) and if at an unseasonable hour, to the Watch-house, there to be confined until the next Morning) who are hereby authorized, upon Proof of the Offence, to commit such Slave or Slaves to the common Goal, for such his, her or their Contempt, and there to remain until the Master, Mistress or Owner of every such Slave or Slaves, shall pay to the Person or Persons who apprehended and committed every such Slave or Slaves, the Sum of *Four Shillings* current Money of *New-York,* for his, her or their pains and Trouble therein, with Reasonable Charges of Prosecution.

And be it further Ordained by the Authority aforesaid, That every Slave or Slaves that shall be convicted of the Offence aforesaid, before he, she or they be discharged out of Custody, shall be Whipped at the Publick Whipping-Post (not exceeding *Forty Lashes*) if desired by the Master or Owner of such Slave or Slaves.

Provided always, and it is the intent hereof, That if two or more Slaves (Not exceeding the Number of Three) be together in any lawful Employ or Labour for the Service of their Master or Mistress (and not otherwise) and only one of them have and carry such Lanthorn with a lighted Candle therein, the other Slaves in such Compay not carrying a Lanthorn and lighted Candle, shall not be construed and intended to be within the meaning and Penalty of this Law, any thing in this Law contained to the contrary hereof in any wise notwithstanding. *Dated at the City-Hall this Two and Twentieth Day of April, in the fourth year of His Majesty's Reign,* Annoq, Domini 1731.

By Order of Common Council,

Will. Sharpas, *Cl.*

Although no laws existed in the early 18th century to protect the rights of free blacks, there were many laws that regulated their conduct. Some of these edicts, like the one shown here, did not even bother to distinguish between a free black and a slave.

ance benefits for family members, assistance for orphans and widows, burial grounds, and basic education in reading, writing, and arithmetic. These organizations, which also sought to protect the rights of free blacks and uplift the race, included the Human and Friendly Society, Minors Moralist, the Friendly Union, the Brown Fellowship Society, and the Society of Free Blacks.

A free black being sold at a slave auction. When free blacks failed to pay their taxes, they could be arrested and, if they still failed to meet their financial obligations, could have their services sold by the sheriff.

Among all these organizations, the churches emerged as the black community's most important institution. But the churches fought an uphill battle. Instead of opposing slavery, white churches supported it. By the 19th century, most southern white Christians had learned to accept slavery even though the practice seemed to contradict their religious doctrines, for slavery made it simple for them to bring Christianity to Africans.

Many white Christians who objected to this rationale, such as the Quakers, left the South. Others, such as the Methodists, gave in to social pressures and supported slavery. Whereas the Methodists had opposed slavery in the late 1700s, they abandoned their arguments against it by 1808, allowing church members and clergy to own slaves with impunity.

The white community besieged black churchgoers with the same restrictions that were placed on all free blacks and their institutions. Black congregations were seldom autonomous. Blacks either worshiped with whites while sitting in a segregated section of the church or worshiped in a church that had been built, owned, and supervised by whites—a kind of branch of the parent church.

The most important aspect of black-white church relations was the degree of white supervision. Charleston had a law against slaves or free blacks congregating for religious purposes without a white person present. Any black who attended such a gathering ran the risk of receiving 20 lashes with a whip. Yet blacks often worshiped secretly, and most of their meetings were held in the evening.

The laws against black church meetings were extreme because the white community dreaded the possibility of a slave revolt. They especially feared a rebellion led by free blacks, and they had good reason to think that such a revolt would grow within a black church, for the church was a place of inspiration. It was also, of course, where the free black community met and organized itself.

White authorities were particularly afraid of free black ministers because they were community leaders. Moreover, they preached about salvation and freedom from the hardships of the slave world. Thus, the potential for revolution lay not only in the assemblage of black churchgoers but in the sermons that black ministers preached.

It was in a black church that Denmark Vesey offered prayers of thanksgiving to God for being delivered out of slavery. Yet he still knew that the bright glow of freedom did not shine on most blacks in America. As a result, he began to believe that God had removed him from slavery for a special mission. He became convinced that his specific purpose in life was to put an end to slavery in America and give to all blacks what was their birthright: the light of freedom. ❦

BARBARY

MEDITERRANEAN SEA

Cyprus

Old Marmora
Tlemsen
ALGIER
TUNIS
Lampadoza
Gerbi
Tripoli

C. Blanco
Mequinez
Saffy
Melaig
Belad el Jerid
al Jerid
Lebida
Sidra in Syrtia
Ras Sem
Derna
Bengazi
Alexandria
Rosetta
Damietta

Madeira
Porto Santo
Desertas

MOROCCO
Morocco
SIJILMISSA
Country of Dates
Wergela
Nadruna
Necani
Gadamis
Gerksa
Wadan

Angela
Barca
Calabathan
Al Bareton
Cairo
Suez

C. de Geer
Santa Cruz

Agare
Sort Desert
Zeghau
Zala
Zaltan Mt.
Siwa
Fauum
EGYPT
Girge
Thebes

Canary I.
Palma
Ferro
Teneriffe
Canary
C. Bojador

Dorodus R. Tatta

GUALATA
Haher
DESERT
Zebbah
Zuela
Mendrah
Mourzouk
Berdoa
Desert of Berdoa
Desert of Lybia
Ombo
Shab

C. Blanco
Menguarts
Wadelims
Labdessebas

SAHARA or Great

Tandeny
Mahbrook
Wadan
KAWAR or KUAR
Salt L. of Damboo
Kanem
KUKU
BARABRA
Selima
Gr. Desert of Chu
DONGOLA

C. C. Mirik
Arguin I.
Hoden

Tisheet Salt M.
Shingarin Salt M.
Aroan S.M.
Fountain
DAR BORNOU
Bornou
Kettocomb
Bir el Malha
Desert Bahiou
Korg
Gerre
Emdurman

Serinpale
St. Louis
Cavor
Oualddo
Dodo
Jarra
Kemnoo
Beroo
BAMBARA
Walet
Tombuctoo
GOTTO
Dibbie L.
BAEDOO
Baghermi
DAR BERGOO
Wara
DAR BAGHERMI
Durli
Zeghawa
Cobbe
Ril
DARFUR
Sem
Tuveldie
KORDOFAN
IBBE

C. Verd
St. Mary
FOULAHS
JALOFFS
Medina
Bambouk
Koombo
KARTA
Kamalia
KAFFABA
KONG
Kaiaba
Kono
Negroes
Bahr Heimad
Biteiah
NEGROES
Copper Mine
NEGROES

Bissagos Is.
FOULAHS
Teemboo
Mount of Kong
DAR KULLA
Bar Kulla
Desert
Bor Junches
Donga
MUJACO
Mount of the Moon

Serra Leona
Shorbra
C. Mesurada
Bassa
DAHOMEY
Abomey
ASHANTEE
Grain Coast
Ivory Coast
Gold Coast
BENIN
WARREE
BIAFRA
Malimbo
CALBONGAS

C. Palmas
St. Andrews R.
C. Formosa
Fernando Po
Bight of Biafra
Congo
St. Benito
Corisco I.

Windward Coast
GULF of GUINEA
Princes I.
St. Thomas

Low Sandy I.

St. Mathews

C. Lopo Gonsalves
Monteng
C. St. Catherine
Nazareth R.

Equinoctial Line

Ambosan I.

Bukameala
Concobella
FUNGENO
LOANGO
LOANGO
Kilongo
Kinghele
Loango
Zahir R.
Angoy
Sundi
St. Salvador
St. Antonio
Nesuata
Bembi
CONGO
Danda
JAGAS

Ascension

St. Paulo de Loanda
ANGOLA
Matamba
R. Coanza
Old Benguela

Rio Longo P.
St. Philip de Benguela
R. St. Francisca
Baca Boa
BEMBE
Quiengo
BUTUA
BORO
Chicova
Tete
Zimbea
MOCARA
Malsea

C. Tarugas
R. Guberer
C. Negro
N.W. Point
Fish B.
M. Fura
SHANGRA
SOF
SAB
INHAMBANI

James Town
St. Helena
the Needles
Georges I.

C. de Ruypis
C. Frio
R. de Angra Fria
CIMBARBAS
BIRI

Praias das Pedras
Farethones
C. Rostro de Pedras
High Land
Walwich Bay
Sandwich Head

Augra Pequena
Pedestal Pt.
Country of the Camelopardalis
CAMDEBO VELD
Delagoa Bay
Orange R.
NAMAQUAS
Copper Mts.
Water Valley
COAST OF NATAL
Port Natal

C. Voltas
Mt. Bramides
Oliphant R.
ANTHON VELD
HOTTENTOTS
Algoa

St. Helens R.
Table Bay
C. Town
Table
C. of Good Hope
First Pt. of
Christophers R.

THE

I

AN

OCEAN

SOUTH

ATLANTIC

5

UNDER THE LASH AND THE NOONDAY SUN

BY THE TIME Denmark Vesey purchased his freedom in 1800, slavery touched every part of black life in the South. This had not always been the case. In 1619, 20 Africans had arrived in the American colonies as indentured servants and were treated much like their European counterparts. Indentured servants were bound by a contract to work for a set period of time, usually five to seven years, until they were able to repay the cost of their passage to the colonies. After their term of service ended, they were free to pursue whatever course they wanted. Many became farmers on land of their own.

As the numbers of independent farmers and craftsmen grew, it became increasingly difficult for the British government to secure indentured servants to fill the need for cheap labor. Before long, a search began for alternative labor sources. As a result, the colonists enslaved such Native Americans as the Pequot, Wampanoag, Nipmuc, and Narragansett of New England and the Creek and Cherokee of the Carolinas. It was relatively easy, however, for Native Americans to escape from their captors and return to their villages.

The bulk of the slave trade in Africa took place in the area known as the Gold Coast, which borders the Gulf of Guinea (middle). Prior to the arrival of the slavers, this region was made up of many prosperous kingdoms.

Eventually, Africa became the major source of labor for the American colonies. Because many Africans were skilled farmers, they needed little training to work on farms and plantations. Africans had also been exposed to Europeans for a longer period of time than Native Americans and had built up immunity to European diseases. In addition, they were easily identifiable and could not escape to the protection of villages the way Native Americans could. And whereas Native Americans were accorded the rights of British subjects (even though they were not granted citizenship), the rights of African slaves were not protected by British law.

Spain, Portugal, and Holland were already importing African slaves to their profitable colonies in the Caribbean and South America when England decided to follow their lead and implement a slave system in the American colonies. By 1650, slavery was well established within all 13 English colonies along the eastern seaboard of North America. To guarantee the continuation of the slave system, colonial governments passed legislation stating that all black newborns would inherit the legal status of their mother. (In England, children inherited their father's status.) Thus, planters and farmers were promised a new supply of slaves, provided their female slaves gave birth.

To justify the enslavement of Africans, the colonists developed racist theories to support their actions. These arguments assumed many forms: Blacks had been cursed by Noah in the Old Testament; they were uncivilized; they were not fully human. Others found justification for slavery because the great ancient civilizations of Greece and Rome had used slaves. Another common argument in favor of slavery was that slave labor provided leisure time for the privileged class to develop new ideas and inventions to improve civilization. Some even argued that because slavery thus facilitated "progress," it actually improved the debased condition of blacks.

To bolster the notion that European colonialists were civilizing blacks, African history was either revised or erased to suit the interests of colonialism. Expunging the history of African kingdoms and civilizations allowed Europeans to categorize Africans as "uncivilized" and "savage." Doing so would not have been possible had they acknowledged the level of culture and civilization that they had found in Africa. Centuries earlier, explorers and traders had marveled at African kingdoms in the western Sudan, which bordered the Gulf of Guinea—the area where much of the early slave trade occurred.

These kingdoms had risen in the medieval period, when Ghana and Mali became great centers of the gold trade. The economic growth of these regions gave rise in the 16th century to the development of strong centralized kingdoms on the south and west coasts of the Sudan. Kingdoms such as Ashanti, Gonja, Akwamu, Dahomey, and Benin grew into prosperous trading centers. By the 19th century, Ashanti had developed into one of the major powers of West Africa. Most traces of African culture, however, were wiped away in the American colonies.

Slavery in America developed differently in the North and in the South, largely because the economies of the regions varied. The southern climate was suitable for growing sugar, tobacco, indigo, rice, and cotton, and southern planters who had the means established large plantations where they could grow vast quantities of these crops. They garnered huge profits largely because they exploited slaves as their primary source of labor.

Because the wealth of the South was concentrated among the large plantation owners, the economy of the South was dependent on slavery. But in the North the economic situation was very different. Northern farms tended to be small and produced a variety of crops that did not demand intense labor, so slave labor never became an integral part of the North's economy.

At the turn of the century, when Denmark Vesey was beginning to contemplate how best to overturn slavery, the United States was undergoing a period of change. The first rumblings of the Industrial Revolution were beginning to be heard. Once again, the North responded to the situation differently than the South did.

In the North, industrialization combined with an influx of poor European immigrants to provide economic deterrents to slavery. It cost less to hire immigrants in the North than it did to purchase slaves and pay for their food, clothing, and shelter. But while the North was rejecting slavery, the South was reviving this "peculiar institution."

In 1793, industrialization came to the South in the form of the cotton gin, which made it easier to separate the cottonseed from the boll of fiber around it. By facilitating the processing of cotton, the gin made growing this crop a profitable business throughout the South and further west, in the undeveloped territories around the Mississippi River. Unlike rice or sugarcane, cotton could be grown throughout the region.

As cotton plantations expanded throughout Georgia, South Carolina, and North Carolina and into the newly formed states of Alabama, Mississippi, and Louisiana, so did the need for slaves. And as the need for slave labor and the value of slaves in the North declined, many northerners freed their slaves or sold them to southern planters for hefty profits. The North even began to outlaw slavery. But this did not happen in the South, where a resurgence in the slave trade was occurring.

South Carolina was no exception to the revival of the slave trade. In 1807, the last year that the slave trade was legal in the United States, the state imported 15,000 Africans into Charleston. Some of the slaves remained in South Carolina after being sold to local buyers. Others went for high prices farther south, in the Cotton Belt states of Georgia, Alabama, and Mississippi.

In the early 1800s, slavery was still regulated by laws that severely circumscribed the activities of the slave population. These laws encroached on every aspect of a slave's life: emotional, cultural, and psychological. Slave codes enacted in Virginia in 1680

The invention of the cotton gin in 1793 led to a cotton boom in the South, and the number of cotton plantations increased dramatically. The demand for slaves to work the fields rose as well, leading to a resurgence of the slave trade in the early 1800s.

had become the model for the entire southern United States. The Virginia codes said:

> No Negro or slave may carry arms.

> If any Negro lift up his hand against any Christian he shall receive thirty lashes.

> If he absent himself or lie out from his master's service and resist lawful apprehension, he may be killed.

The Virginia codes provided the starting point for legislation, but in most cases in the 1800s the laws were more specific and far-reaching. In Charleston, slaves could not leave the plantation without a written pass from their master or mistress. Like free blacks, they could not testify against whites in court, only against blacks. And though the killing of a slave by a white person was seldom dealt with as murder, a slave could not strike a white person, even in self-defense. Those convicted of crimes could be burned alive.

In South Carolina, slaves could not travel without a pass unless accompanied by a white. Slaves who left home without permission were whipped. Nor were they allowed to trade without the consent of their owner.

All plantations had to have a white person in residence, if not the master or a member of the family, then at least a white overseer who was hired to supervise the slaves. Unless they were household servants or coach drivers, slaves were given only coarse clothing to wear: woolen suits and shirts and dresses made of cotton or linen.

In Charleston, slaves and free blacks had to wear identification tags. Embossed on these brass badges were the name of the city of Charleston, an identification number, and, if it applied, the word *free*. Free blacks had to put their occupation on their badge. Slaves who were hired out had to display their oc-

Free blacks and slaves were forced by law to wear brass identification tags. Each tag contained information denoting the person's free or slave status, occupation, and identification number as well as the year.

cupation, the name of their owner, and the year. According to a city ordinance in Charleston, a slave received 39 lashes and was placed in the stocks for 1 hour if found wearing the badge of a free black.

Such laws were designed not only to legislate the subordinate status of the slave but also to thwart slave rebellions. At the turn of the century, white southerners had good reason to fear an uprising. In 1791, slaves and free blacks on the French island of St. Domingue, spurred on by the rhetoric of the French Revolution, began a revolt of their own.

In 1793, France abolished slavery within its territories, but it did little to stop the revolution on St. Domingue, which was as much about the rights of free blacks as it was about ending slavery. The island remained in a state of armed revolt for 10 more years.

In the 1800s, South Carolina's white community executed slaves and free blacks convicted of serious crimes. Burning a man alive was one of the more barbarous methods of execution employed in such cases.

Then, in 1804, the revolutionary forces won their independence and named their new republic Haiti.

Although Americans were proud that their revolution had influenced the one in France, the news of a successful black revolt and the creation of an independent black nation terrified white southerners. They were especially fearful because throughout the turmoil in St. Domingue, white refugees had fled to the South, and many of them brought along their slaves. Southern whites were sure that word of the revolution on St. Domingue would spread throughout the region's slave population.

South Carolina began taking in French refugees as early as 1792. As a steady flow of refugees continued in the years that followed, Joseph Vesey became treasurer of a committee formed to aid the fleeing colonists. It is likely that while these refugees were visiting the former captain on King Street, their slaves discussed the events taking place on St. Domingue with Denmark.

Like other southern states, South Carolina passed laws to try to keep free blacks and slaves ignorant of the revolution in Haiti. In 1793, following an attempted slave rebellion in Norfolk, Virginia, South Carolina's governor mandated that all free blacks and people of color who had come from St. Domingue during the previous year had to leave the state within 10 days. In addition, French refugees from St. Domingue who came to the United States were no longer permitted to bring their slaves.

The precautions taken to suppress news about the Haitian revolution failed. Literate slaves could read about Haiti in newspaper articles and editorials. Slaves in southern cities such as Charleston—especially those who worked in white households—overheard conversations about the revolt.

When Denmark Vesey heard about the rebellion, he was secretly pleased. He knew that whites were still justifying the practice of slavery by arguing that it not only benefited the black population but was the most favorable condition under which black and white people could coexist. He also heard it said that a slave was better off than a northern laborer who had to work long hours for paltry wages.

In Joseph Vesey's household, Denmark Vesey had been in the company of slaves and free blacks with whom he discussed the issues of slavery, freedom, and rebellion. After he was freed, he shared his opinions with the free blacks he met in church and elsewhere. He also befriended the slaves whom he encountered

during his travels throughout Charleston County as a carpenter. He listened carefully to them so he could learn what was going on not only in Charleston but also throughout the United States and the Caribbean.

While the white and black communities of Charleston were following the news from St. Domingue, insurrection threatened much closer to home. In the spring of 1800, 2 slaves, Gabriel Prosser and Jack Bowler, stockpiled clubs, swords, and other crude weapons and planned a rebellion of more than 1,000 slaves. Their aim was to attack the city of Richmond, Virginia. On August 30, 1800, the slaves assembled six miles outside of Richmond. A violent storm interrupted their march, however, and allowed

Blacks battle French colonialists on St. Domingue during the slave rebellion that led to the creation of the black republic of Haiti in 1804. Vesey modeled his plans for a slave uprising on this successful revolt.

state officials, who had been warned in advance of the plot by two slaves, to assemble a large number of troops. The authorities promptly arrested the rebellious slaves and executed 35 of them, putting an end to the revolt.

Throughout the South, rumors of plots continued to arise constantly, and so did the vigilance of whites. Whenever a fire began blazing or a white met an untimely death, the cause was often attributed to slaves wreaking revenge. While the South argued to its northern detractors that blacks were happy as slaves, southern planters watched carefully for signs of resistance. And, in truth, slaves were constantly resisting—by surviving.

In a world in which rules and regulations governed their lives, slaves always used their intelligence, creativity, and common sense to ensure their physical and psychological well-being. For example, slaves were not allowed to play the drums, which had served as the foundation of their music. As a substitute, they used hand clapping and foot stomping to accompany their singing. Drums had also played an integral part in Africa in a system of long-distance communication. Slaves, deprived of their drums for communication, sang songs whose lyrics had double meanings—a kind of secret code.

Slaves could not legally marry. Yet they developed close family ties among blood relatives and adopted kin, continued the African tradition of naming children after grandparents, and observed African taboos against marriage between cousins. Denmark Vesey reportedly had several wives who were slaves.

Teaching a slave to read and write was illegal, but this law was also difficult to enforce. Skilled slaves, including Denmark Vesey, learned how to read in order to practice their trade. Those slaves and free blacks who could read secretly taught others to do so.

Not all slave owners enforced slave codes and rules in the same way, however, which meant that the lives of slaves depended on the personality of their master and the occupation of the slave. In this respect, Denmark Vesey had been lucky. During his years as a slave, he had not experienced the worst of slave life because he had been a skilled slave, a carpenter who controlled much of his own time and his own work. Even before he became a carpenter in Charleston, Vesey had little firsthand knowledge of the hardships of plantation life. Instead of working in the hot sun on a plantation in the Caribbean or the American South, he had sailed the Atlantic as the personal slave of a sea captain.

Nevertheless, those voyages across the Atlantic, along with the Charleston slave auctions, provided sufficient motivation for Denmark Vesey to rise up against slavery. Surrounded by a system that degraded human beings, he became a champion of civil rights for his people. It made no difference that he had achieved his own freedom. Vesey felt that no one should be a slave. No child should be taken away from his or her parents. No husband should be taken away from his wife, and no wife should be taken away from her husband. No man, woman, or child should work and receive nothing in return. And people should not be whipped, tortured, and worked to death merely because of the color of their skin. ✿

6

A MAN OF
CONVICTION

INITIALLY, DENMARK VESEY did not plan any specific action to combat slavery. Instead, he launched an intellectual crusade. He read all that he could about slavery, about the American and French revolutions, about Haitian independence. He learned that the American Revolution was supposed to have been about "unalienable rights" and that in France the rallying cry had been "Liberté, Egalité, Fraternité" (Liberty, Equality, Brotherhood). Haiti's independence made him rejoice.

Vesey also listened to southerners rail against the growing antislavery movement, a small but vocal minority that wanted to destroy slavery—some by moral persuasion, others by violence. This prompted him to study the pamphlets issued by abolitionists and to read them to his friends. He examined the appeals of black abolitionists who argued not only for the end of slavery in the South but for black equality. He listened as proslavery southerners developed their theory of "positive good," arguing that slavery helped create a better society than did paid labor in the

In the early 1800s, free blacks often discussed how to better their political situation in public gatherings. Vesey began formulating his plans for a revolt by voicing his opinions at these informal meetings.

The issue of slavery was hotly debated in Congress well before the onset of the Civil War. Vesey closely followed the newspaper accounts of these debates and became convinced by what he read—that Congress supported his goal of abolishing slavery.

North. Vesey carefully analyzed all that he read, overheard, and discussed. He formulated theories as he studied the world of Charleston and the role of slavery in that world.

In 1820, Charleston was the sixth largest city in the United States. The black population of the city exceeded the white population; there were 13,652

New York senator Rufus King was one of the abolitionists who inspired Vesey in his fight for black rights. Vesey most likely heard about King through newspaper accounts of his activities.

slaves and 1,475 free blacks, but only 10,654 whites. In fact, blacks outnumbered whites by a small margin statewide. Yet slaves and free blacks held no power in South Carolina, and their numbers made whites all the more fearful of a potential uprising.

The rebellion led by Gabriel Prosser, Haiti's independence, abolitionist propaganda, and crimes attributed to slaves added to the fears of white southerners. Patrols were established in all districts of South Carolina to prevent slave rebellions. Slave owners in each district had to serve on patrol duty. They were required to serve in the militia after they turned 18. Female slave owners and those unwilling

Although many people in the North advocated the end of slavery, 100 of the 130 abolitionist societies founded in the United States before 1827 were located in the South. Among the most outspoken abolitionists were the sisters Sarah (right) and Angelina Grimké (opposite), both of whom were residents of Charleston.

or unable to serve could pay for a substitute. Anyone who failed to serve or to provide someone to take their place was fined.

As a member of the free black community, Denmark Vesey was as vulnerable to white hostilities as any other black, and perhaps even more so. The positive-good theory of slavery included the assumption that good masters created good slaves who were happy and content. Thus, the danger of insurrection lay within the free black community, not within the community of slaves, who were assumed to be loyal and obedient.

The church that Denmark Vesey attended, like other black churches, became a primary target for whites who feared the free black community. The

whites who headed Charleston's Methodist church took away the black congregation's right to meet on its own. Morris Brown, the minister of the black congregation, led a secession from the white church, deciding with the other black members to form their own church, the Hampstead African Church.

Brown was not the first black minister to take such action. In 1787, Richard Allen had taken similar measures in Philadelphia, where he and other black parishioners left St. George's Methodist Episcopal Church in a protest against discriminatory practices and formed their own congregation in Bethel Church. In 1816, Bethel joined with other independent black Methodist congregations in the Northeast to organize a new denomination, the African

Methodist Episcopal church. So in 1817, when Brown and his followers organized the African Association in Charleston, they were following the example set by the African Methodist Episcopal church.

Denmark Vesey belonged to the Hampstead African Church, which was located just outside of Charleston. Shortly after Brown founded the Hampstead Church, 469 black worshipers were falsely ac-

Blacks in the North were extremely active in the abolitionist movement and held conventions such as this one in Washington, D.C., to help bring about the end of slavery. They also sought to stop the treatment of blacks as second-class citizens in nonslave states.

cused and arrested for disorderly conduct. Then, on a Sunday morning in June of the following year, another 140 Hampstead worshipers were put in jail. The city council convicted a bishop and four ministers from the group and gave them two choices: Spend an entire month in jail or leave the state. The city council also sentenced 8 ministers to receive 10 lashes or pay $10 each.

ANTI-SLAVERY WAFERS,

Designed to further the Cause of Emancipation, by continually exposing the Sin of Slavery.

Price One Halfpenny, or Three Shillings per 100. Published by H. Armour, 54 South Bridge, Edinburgh.

A man may sell himself to work for another, but he cannot sell himself to be a slave. *Blackstone.*	All men are created free and equal, and have an inalienable right to liberty. *Fundamental Principle of American Government.*	He that holds another man as property, is more detestable than the robber and the assasin combined. *Thomas Day, 1776.*	The negroes are destitute of the Gospel, and ever will be, under the present state of things.—*Synod of South Carolina and Georgia, 1834.*	ANTI-SLAVERY. The righteous considereth the cause of the poor: but the wicked regardeth not to know it. *Prov. xxix. 7.*
Those are man-stealers who abduct, keep, sell, or buy slaves. *Grotius, 1650.*	Men-buyers are exactly on a level with Men-stealers. *Rev. J. Wesley, 1777.*	Slaves are liable, as chattels, to be sold by the master at his pleasure, and may be taken in execution for debt. *Kentucky Law of Descent.*	To be a slave, is to be denied the privilege of reading the Gospel of the Son of God. *Elijah P. Lovejoy, 1837.*	Shall the throne of iniquity have fellowship with thee, which frameth mischief by a law. *Psalm xciv. 20.*
Slaveholding is injustice which no considerations of policy can extenuate. *Bishop Horsley, 1785.*	I thought it my duty to expose the monstrous impiety and cruelty, not only of the slave-trade, but of slave-holding itself, in whatever form it is found. *Gran. Sharpe, 1787.*	Time has proved that slavery and education are incompatible." *Cassius M. Clay, 1845.*	To be a slave, is to be shut out from all enjoyment in this world, and all hope in the next. *Elijah P. Lovejoy, 1837.*	Anti-slavery.— Who will stand up for me against the evil-doers, or who will stand up for me against the workers of iniquity. *Psalm xciv. 16.*
Man-stealers! the worst of thieves: in comparison of whom, highway robbers and housebreakers are innocent. *Rev. J. Wesley, 1777.*	Liberty is the right of every human creature as soon as he breathes the vital air; and no human law can deprive him of that right. *Rev. J. Wesley, 1777.*	All meetings of slaves, at any meeting-house or school, for learning to read or write, shall be deemed unlawful. *Virginia Code, 1819.*	Negroes are not free agents, have no personal liberty, no faculty of acquiring property, but are themselves property, at the will of their masters. *Patterson, in Convent. 1787.*	ANTI-SLAVERY. Woe unto him that useth his neighbour's service without wages, and giveth him not for his work. *Jer. xxii. 13.*
The children of men are by nature free, and cannot without injustice be either reduced to or held in slavery. *Judge Jay, 1786.*	The owners of slaves are licensed robbers, and not the just proprietors of what they claim. *Mr. Rice, Kentucky, 1780.*	The Christian religion classes man-stealers with murderers of fathers and mothers. *Bishop Porteous.*	Why ought slavery to be abolished? Because it is incurable injustice. *William Pitt.*	ANTI-SLAVERY. THOU SHALT NOT STEAL. *Ex. xx. 15.*
The Almighty God has no attribute that can take sides with Slaveholders. *Thomas Jefferson.*	To hold a man in slavery is to be every day guilty of robbing him of his liberty, or of manstealing. *Jonathan Edwards, 1791.*	He that stealeth a man, and selleth him, or if he be found in his hand, he shall surely be put to death. *Exodus xxi. 16*	Let sorrow bathe each blushing cheek, Bend piteous o'er the tortured slave, Whose wrongs compassion cannot speak, Whose only refuge is the grave. *Mrs. Morton.*	There are Three Millions of Slaves in the United States of Christian (?) America.
ANTI-SLAVERY. Be not partakers of other men's sins.	ANTI-SLAVERY. Remember them that are in bonds as bound with them. *Heb. xiii. 3.*	Anti-slavery.—Love worketh no ill to his neighbour, therefore Love is the fulfilling of the Law. *Rom. xiii. 10.*	ANTI-SLAVERY. God hath made of one blood all nations. *Acts xvii. 26.*	Is not every slave a brother or a sister, ought we not then to seek for immediate, universal, and unconditional EMANCIPATION.
Anti-slavery. Where the Spirit of the Lord is, there is liberty. *2 Cor. iii. 17.*	Proclaim liberty to the captive, and the opening of the prison doors to them that are bound. *Isaiah lxi. 1.*	Pure religion and undefiled before God and the Father is this, to visit the fatherless and the widows in their affliction, and to keep himself unspotted from the world.	Anti-slavery. Whatsoever ye would that men should do unto you, do ye even so to them. *Matt. vii. 12.*	Oppression is the forerunner of revolution, are not Slaveholders then tampering with the internal peace of America?
Anti-slavery. Woe unto him that buildeth his house by unrighteousness. *Bible.*	Every slaveholder is guilty of reducing human beings to the condition of brutes and things.	All who fellowship with slaveholders are abettors and promoters of theft, robbery, and concubinage.	There is no respect of persons with God. *Rom. ii. 11.* In the churches of the U. S. separate pews are generally provided for the negroes.	The slave can do nothing, possess nothing, nor acquire anything but what must belong to his master. *Louisiana Civil Code.*
There are Seven Millions of Slaves in the World, held by professedly Christian nations	Anti-slavery. In Christian America there is no Marriage for the Slaves.	In American Slaves are joined to Churches, as members, to enhance their price on the auction-block.	Thou shalt love thy neighbour as thyself. *Matthew, xxii. 39.*	In America 80,000 slaves are members of the Presbyterian Church, and these men and women have no legal marriage.
NO UNION with SLAVEHOLDERS.	Is not this the fast that I have chosen, to loose the bands of wickedness, to undo the heavy burdens, and to let the oppressed go free, and that ye break every yoke.	Is every Free Church to have a SLAVE STONE in it?—*Rev. Dr. Duncan of the Free Church.*	Slaves shall be deemed, held, taken, reputed, and judged in law to be chattels personal. *South Carolina Code.*	Every slave in America is a stolen man or woman—every slaveholder is a man-stealer.
While men despise *fraud*, and loathe *rapine*, and abhor *blood*, they shall reject with indignation the wild and guilty phantasy, that man can hold property in man. *Brougham.*	My God what wish can prosper, or what prayer, For those who deal in cargoes of despair; Or drive a loathsome traffic, gauge and span, And buy the muscles and the bones of man. *Cowper.*	Are we then fanatics? Are we enthusiasts? Because we say to all Slaveholders, Do not rob, Do not murder. *Charles James Fox.*	Have we separated ourselves from our moderate brethren to form an alliance with manstealers. *Rev. B. Grey, Moderator of the Free Church General Assembly for 1846.*	Slaves regard all instruction, addressed especially to themselves, as a device of their masters, to make them more obedient and profitable to them. Such are the workings of slavery.

One of the ways that abolitionists got their message to the public was through the use of envelope seals. Known as wafers, these seals bore antislavery quotations that were taken from the Bible as well as from prominent philosophers and statesmen.

In 1820, a group of free blacks from the Hampstead African Church petitioned the Charleston legislature to allow the church to hold services without white supervision. The petition was promptly denied. Nevertheless, the Hampstead African Church continued to hold services until 1822, when attempts to suppress the church grew so great that it could not withstand them.

Some free blacks decided to give in to the white authorities and tried to create a black community in which privilege was based on wealth and loyalty to the white community. The people who made up this community were far more likely to inform on the local black population than to help it resist slavery and inequality. Some of the informers had white fathers who had provided them with an education, money, and property. Some were favored servants who had been rewarded with manumission as well as money and property. Others were skilled laborers who had accumulated money and property through their hard work and good reputation.

One group of free blacks took an even more extreme route. Abandoning all hope that the United States would ever confer on them equal rights, this group decided to leave the United States and return to Africa. In 1820, the black Methodist missionary Daniel Coker helped establish a settlement of black Americans in Sierra Leone, West Africa. By 1830, as many as 1,420 former slaves had relocated to West Africa.

Denmark Vesey joined neither of these factions. He was determined to do whatever he could to help all black people become free, to end slavery forever. He knew he could not accomplish his goal if he held himself aloof from other blacks, whether they were slaves or free, dark or light, successful or destitute. There was nothing he could do to end slavery if he

emigrated to Africa. He chose instead to remain in the United States and fight for his people.

For men and women with convictions like those of Denmark Vesey, the slave and free black communities were inseparable. Denmark refused to abandon his slave neighbors in the Neck and those slaves who continued to toil in the ever-expanding cotton fields of the South. He wanted to be the Moses of his people, to release them from bondage and lead them to a promised land of freedom.

As the years passed, Denmark Vesey became intensely committed to his mission. His character was perfectly suited to the role he was looking to fulfill.

He was assertive and arrogant. He thought a great deal of himself and his abilities. He talked openly about black rights when it was imprudent to do so. He enjoyed challenging whites by debating racial issues in public. Whereas few blacks dared argue with whites about anything, especially racial issues, Denmark Vesey publicly challenged the slave system. He intentionally started arguments with whites, sometimes in an effort to find white sympathizers, sometimes simply to show other blacks that it could be done. Whatever his reasons and motives, he had the nerve to confront the white community and display his considerable intelligence.

The majority of Charleston's black community thought Vesey was either terribly brave or extremely stupid. Still, his boldness earned their respect and admiration. But at the same time, they feared the retaliation of the white community. ✦

In the early 1820s, minister Morris Brown (above) formed his own black church, the Hampstead African Church. In doing so, he followed the example of Richard Allen (opposite), who established the African Methodist Episcopal Church in 1816.

7

A PLAN
FOR FREEDOM

IN 1821, DENMARK VESEY decided on his course of action. He would organize other blacks who were committed to the fight against slavery, and together they would form an army. Vesey planned for this army to kill slave owners and destroy their property, thus beginning a revolt that would free slaves not only in Charleston but throughout the United States.

Vesey began to carry out his plan by observing the people he thought were best equipped to join him as leaders of an insurrection. The members of this small, loyal group would serve as his chief lieutenants. They would help him develop strategies for recruiting supporters, raising money, collecting ammunition and weapons, and organizing volunteers. He looked for men who were trustworthy, articulate, and well respected. He also sought out those who had occupations or ties within the community that would be of use to the rebellion.

Vesey addresses a gathering at Charleston's Hampstead African Church, where he occasionally held meetings to discuss his plans for a slave revolt. The size of these meetings was usually small, to preserve secrecy.

By December 1821, Vesey had completed his research and was ready to select his cadre of lieutenants. He had already devised specific assignments for each of the six men he would choose. The assignments reflected several important concerns that the 54-year-old Vesey harbored about the organization of the insurrection.

Vesey preferred to recruit slaves who hired out their services, such as the ones shown here. He knew from his own experience that they not only had some control over their time and movements but also possessed a small amount of savings that they might contribute to the cause.

Communication between the conspirators in the city and those on plantations was one of Vesey's particular concerns. He knew that any communication between these two groups would be especially difficult. The occupations of urban slaves often gave them freedom of movement, but plantation owners kept track of every movement of their slaves.

In plotting his rebellion, Vesey believed he could trust rural slaves and plantation field hands who showed no attachment to their owners. His recruiting efforts stretched into rural South Carolina and also went beyond the state's borders.

Vesey needed someone who could secretly pass information to plantation slaves who had joined the revolt, and he recognized that a slave named Peter Poyas possessed the qualities needed for such a delicate job. Poyas was a ship's carpenter, and he was literate. Like other skilled slaves, his work allowed him to travel all over Charleston without suspicion. Poyas managed to recruit 600 volunteers from the Charleston area and kept a comprehensive list of all their names.

Vesey also recognized that Rolla and Ned Bennett would be very useful. They were slaves in Governor Thomas Bennett's household. Thus, they were in an ideal position to spy on the white community and to obtain information about political and social events in Charleston. To make matters even better, both men seemed to be above suspicion.

The rebels also needed a treasurer. For this position, Vesey picked another literate and skilled slave, a painter named Jack Glenn. Vesey and Glenn were both well aware from their own experience that slaves who were hired out received an allowance and thus had some disposable income. Glenn collected money from these slaves to purchase weapons and horses. Vesey, whose property was reportedly worth $8,000 at the time of his death, doubtless contributed funds to the rebellion.

Vesey also recruited Monday Gell, who made harnesses at his master's livery stable. His connection to the stable would, Vesey hoped, help the rebels commandeer horses when the time came. Like the other lieutenants, Gell was highly regarded within the white community yet trusted by the black community. He was said to be a likable person, known for his intelligence, sobriety, and dependability. Gell was one of the last to join Denmark Vesey's small inner circle.

Vesey recognized that his movement needed spiritual guidance of a kind that he could not give. He needed someone who could offer the revolt's followers an uncompromising belief in their ability to succeed in spite of overwhelming odds. This person had to be a leader in the black community—someone who could rally the timid and the insecure. Vesey chose Jack Pritchard, who was known as Gullah Jack because he came from the isolated slave communities on the coastal islands near Charleston. These slaves, Kongo people of Angolan descent, were called the Gullah.

Gullah Jack proved indispensable to the revolt. For those who were skeptical and hesitant, the presence of Gullah Jack made the impossible seem possible. Gullah Jack was said to be a conjurer, a person known among the Kongo people to possess the gift of being able to manipulate the world through his knowledge of spiritual forces and nature.

Whereas Vesey's followers shared his vision of freedom and feared his bold, aggressive personality, Gullah Jack appealed to the black community for a different reason. People thought of him as invincible. They feared him not because of what he thought and said but because of what he could achieve with his powers. Vesey's boldness might have seemed a bit foolhardy at times, but it was impossible to argue with Gullah Jack. Vesey had intellect, but Gullah Jack had intuition. And where Vesey was brave, Gullah Jack could be cruel. Together they made quite a team.

In effect, Vesey chose two types of leaders. Most, like Ned and Rolla Bennett, were so well regarded by the white community that they would not be suspected. Others, like Gullah Jack and Vesey himself, were so well respected by the black community that their commitment to the plan would never be in doubt. All of these men were willing to use any means necessary to achieve their desired ends.

Vesey strictly warned his followers against recruiting domestic servants. He believed that these slaves were loyal to their owners and could not be trusted.

When Vesey's lieutenants were in place, the business of recruiting began in earnest. He instructed his lieutenants to look for slaves who were skilled, literate, and had some degree of mobility. He advised against using slaves who were too attached to their masters, and he was particularly suspicious of house servants. Yet urban house slaves in Charleston were in the best position to carry out the intricate plot. They had already gained the trust of their masters and were allowed to travel around town without suspicion. As a result, Vesey needed the very slaves he distrusted, and so it was necessary for him to enlist a few carefully chosen domestic servants.

The slaves that Vesey felt he could trust implicitly were the Gullah and those who had lived in the

Caribbean. Many of these slaves lived in relative isolation and managed to escape the influences of American and European culture. Instead, they maintained much of their African culture, including its language, art, cooking, and religion. Vesey took for granted the loyalty of these slaves to his revolt against Charleston and recruited them heavily.

The recruitment operation extended well beyond Charleston. As well as covering the coastal islands, recruiters reportedly enlisted followers as far east as Georgetown. To the north, the effort reached St.

Marsh Island, off the coast of Charleston, was one of the main areas where Vesey looked for loyal supporters because most of the slaves who lived there maintained their ties to African culture.

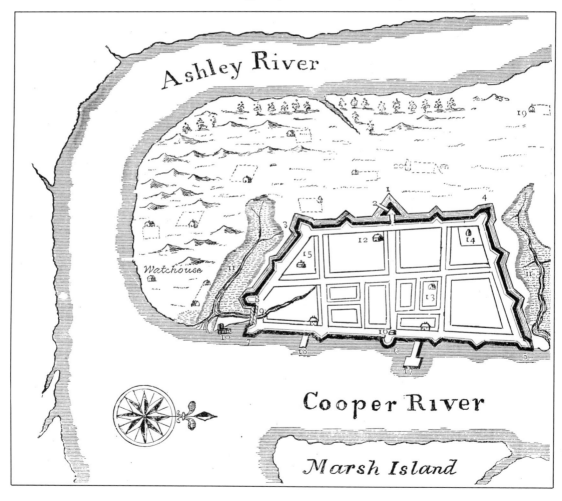

John's Parish in Berkeley County. And other followers came from as far west as the Combahee River.

For security reasons, each recruit was to know
only the name of the man who had been his initial
contact. At small meetings in Vesey's house on Bull
Street, the lieutenants reported the number of recruits on each list, but no names were given. These
precautions meant that if a person was caught, the
authorities would have no way of identifying the other
members of the conspiracy, and the plans could con-
tinue. Relying on the strategy of a surprise attack,
Vesey thought it essential to employ methods that
maintained absolute secrecy.

By March 1822, Vesey had begun to work full-
time on his plans for revolt. He held secret meetings
at his house and at a farm in the Neck. He kept the
meetings small to prevent detection and to maintain
a high degree of anonymity among his followers in
the case of betrayal by a fellow conspirator.

Church meetings soon turned into surreptitious
planning sessions as well. Several of Vesey's lieutenants, including Gullah Jack and Monday Gell, were
members with Vesey of the Hampstead African
Church; Ned Bennett and Peter Poyas were "class
leaders." They were responsible for the Christian conduct of church members assigned to them and acted
as spiritual and administrative guides for the church
during weekly prayer meetings and on those Sundays
when their minister visited his other congregations.
Meetings between class leaders and church members
provided an excellent opportunity to discuss ways to
improve the status of blacks.

Denmark Vesey used his own meetings to inspire
and indoctrinate. He had read widely about commitment, struggle, and self-respect and called on his
vast knowledge of the Bible, Greek mythology, and
American history to bolster his arguments. His chief
line of reasoning was very basic: If whites would not

While planning his uprising, Vesey wrote to Jean-Pierre Boyer, president of Haiti, to enlist his aid. Vesey believed that once his forces had control of Charleston, Boyer would send troops to expand the scope of the revolution.

give blacks the freedom that was rightfully theirs, then blacks would have to take it forcefully. He likened the fight for black freedom to the release from bondage that the Hebrews had achieved with God's help centuries earlier. He also reminded his followers that Haiti had won its independence through the power of the sword, and he quoted Scripture at planning meetings to demonstrate that God was the power behind the sword when it was raised for a righteous cause:

> And I am sure that the king of Egypt will not let you go, no, not by a mighty hand.
> And I will stretch out my hand, and smite Egypt with all my wonders which I will do in the midst thereof: and after that he will let you go (Exodus 3:19–20).

Vesey not only read from the Bible but quoted newspapers, antislavery pamphlets, the Constitution of the United States, and the Declaration of Independence. There was much in the latter document for him to refer to, especially the opening passages:

> We hold these truths to be self-evident, that all men are created equal, that they are endowed by their Creator with certain unalienable Rights, that among these are Life, Liberty, and the pursuit of Happiness.—That to secure these rights, Governments are instituted among Men, deriving their just powers from the consent of the governed,—that whenever any Form of Government becomes destructive of these ends, it is the Right of the People to alter or to abolish it, and to institute new Government, laying its foundation on such principles and organizing its powers in such form, as to them shall seem most likely to effect their Safety and Happiness.

Although Vesey believed that the providential hand of God would help him win the battle, he did not expect a miracle. He thought that God would assist those who, like the rebels in Haiti, took the first step toward freedom. Indeed, if blacks would only unite to fight oppression, then a revolt in Charleston might very well mark the beginning of a global struggle to win black liberation.

With these ideas in mind, Vesey sought the help of Haitian president Jean-Pierre Boyer. Vesey wrote a letter to the president that expressed these thoughts and gave it to a cook on a ship bound for Haiti. He told the cook to make sure that it was delivered to Boyer.

While Vesey awaited the Haitian president's promise of aid, he also believed—erroneously, as it turned out—that he had the support of the federal government. He relied on newspaper accounts of congressional speeches and public debates, which were often misleading or inaccurate, for information on what was going on in the nation. When a debate was held in Congress on the admission of Missouri to the Union as a free state, Vesey mistakenly heard that the government had freed all slaves west of the Mississippi but that their owners would not comply with the government's edict. Freedom, he told his followers, would come only through bloodshed.

These particulars meant little to Vesey's lieutenants and followers. They did not need any more convincing. They simply went to the meetings to make plans for the revolt.

At these meetings, collections were taken to purchase arms and other necessities. With the money that they amassed, a local blacksmith was able to make bayonets—300 by the time of the revolt. This cache of weapons was hidden in the Neck. In addition, each of Vesey's lieutenants had his own weapon—a sword, dagger, pistol, or musket—ready for the appointed hour. ❦

8

TO STRIKE A BLOW
FOR FREEDOM

D URING THE SPRING of 1822, the wealthy residents of Charleston were busy planning their summer vacations. When the summer months arrived, they headed north to escape the heat, confident that while they were away their slaves would take care of all matters at home. But nothing could have been further from the truth.

Denmark Vesey ordinarily believed that slaves should not degrade themselves in front of whites. He hated to see blacks defer to anyone. But during the months prior to the scheduled revolt, he encouraged his followers to be submissive and obedient in order to place the whites off guard. Lulling the white community into a sense of complacency was bound to ensure the secrecy of the conspiracy.

Vesey had set the date of the attack for Sunday, July 14, 1822. The planters who were enjoying the cooler weather in such places as New York and Boston were to be the lucky ones. Vesey had instructed his troops to kill all whites without exception. They were also told to kill any black who had sided with the white community. This was the strategy that had worked on St. Domingue, and Vesey believed it would work in Charleston.

Vesey anticipated that the streets of Charleston would be quiet in July 1822. The city's elite always vacationed in the North during the summer months, making it an ideal time to launch an attack against the white community.

Vesey instructed his followers to be especially agreeable to whites in the months preceding the revolt. He hoped that the seeming obedience of the slaves would lull the white community into a sense of complacency.

But one of Vesey's men made a mistake. On May 25, a Saturday, William Paul, one of Vesey's followers, happened to see Peter Prioleau at the Charleston wharf. Prioleau, a house slave who belonged to Colonel John C. Prioleau, was returning from the fish market and had stopped to look at a schooner anchored in the harbor when he was approached by

Paul. In the course of their conversation, Paul told Prioleau about the uprising and invited him to join the army of slaves. But Prioleau was not the least bit interested—he did not resent his work or his position in a white household. In fact, he was completely loyal to his master. Alarmed by what he heard, he took leave of Paul as quickly as he could, afraid of being seen with a conspirator.

Prioleau was precisely the kind of person whom Vesey and Peter Poyas feared could betray the revolt. Poyas had been careful to warn recruiters of this danger. He had told them not to mention the uprising to slaves who got on well with their masters.

On the fateful day that Paul broke the rules of recruitment, Prioleau's master was out of town. Yet Prioleau was so frightened by his knowledge of the impending revolt that he told one of Colonel Prioleau's sons what Paul had said to him. He then sought the advice of a neighbor, a free black named William Pencil, who advised him to tell the colonel as soon as possible.

Colonel Prioleau did not return home until May 30. But he acted quickly once he was told about the plot. He notified the mayor, who called the city council into an emergency session. The council interrogated Peter Prioleau and determined from his answers that Paul was the organizer of the revolt. He was brought before the council to be questioned. At first, Paul denied any knowledge of a rebellion. But after a night of interrogation, which undoubtedly featured some extreme methods to elicit his cooperation, he confessed and implicated others in the conspiracy.

Because of Paul's testimony, Peter Poyas and Mingo Harth were arrested that very day, May 31. But both Poyas and Harth played dumb when being questioned by the mayor and members of the city council. Poyas shrugged his shoulders and burst into a loud, buffoonish laugh. When a council member

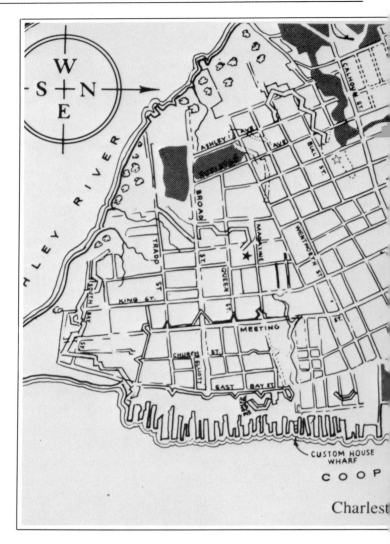

shouted at him to stop laughing and to answer the
questions, Harth poked Poyas in the ribs. Then they
both started laughing, poking at each other, playfully
hitting each other on the back, telling each other to
stop laughing and to answer the question.

Poyas and Harth saved their lives by convincing
the mayor and the city council that they were too
ignorant to be involved in a conspiracy. No evidence

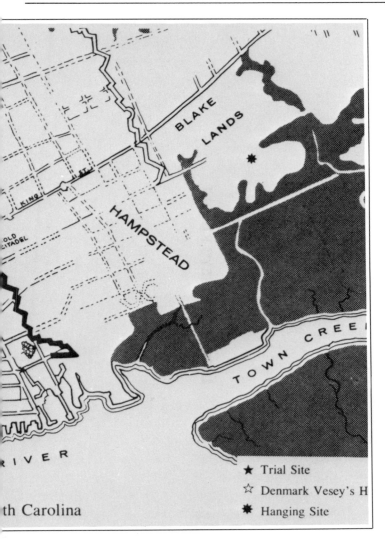

★ Trial Site

☆ Denmark Vesey's H

✳ Hanging Site

th Carolina

Vesey's plan for a slave rebellion called for a five-point attack on Charleston. Vesey himself would lead a party from his house (located at white star, center) to the guardhouse across from St. Michael's Church at the intersection of Meeting and Broad streets (lower left).

to incriminate them was found among their personal property, and they were released. Vesey had acted correctly in choosing Poyas and Mingo to serve as his lieutenants. The white community trusted them completely.

But the authorities took no chances. To guard against the slightest possibility of a slave revolt, the city council hired a few men to carefully watch Poyas and Harth, even though the authorities found it hard to believe that slaves were planning to destroy Charleston. It seemed too frightening to be true.

When the other blacks named by Paul were brought before the city council for questioning, they handled themselves with such composure that the authorities had no choice but to let them go, too. Yet they were all followed as soon as they were released and were watched for any sign of suspicious activity.

Major John Wilson, a Charleston resident, went one step further than the authorities. He asked one of his mother's most trusted slaves, George Wilson, to spy for him and find out if an insurrection was brewing. A class leader in church, George found out from some fellow slaves at church that a rebellion was indeed being planned. When this new piece of information about an uprising reached Governor Thomas Bennett, he called for an increase in military forces and for more arms to be stored in the city arsenals. Guards were posted around the city.

As soon as Vesey found out that some of his men had been hauled before the authorities, he began to fear the treachery of an informant. Consequently, he decided that his best course of action was to set an earlier date for the rebellion. He chose Sunday, June 16. He had no way of informing all the volunteers of the change, however. He would have to hope that word of mouth would get the news to enough of the rebels.

Everything else appeared to be ready. The weapons were all in place, and Vesey's lieutenants had identified the location of arms and ammunition in arsenals, guardhouses, and armories throughout Charleston. The revolutionaries planned on opening the militia's depository and taking as many as 300 guns. They would steal 500 more from Duquercron's gun shop. Gunsmiths' shops and an arsenal across from St. Michael's Church would also be raided.

The plan called for a five-point attack, with a separate patrol on horseback. Each of Vesey's lieutenants was given a specific assignment. Poyas volunteered for the most dangerous assignment: He would lead a party to the main guardhouse and seize the arsenal there. Ned Bennett would command an attack made up of slaves from the countryside and the Neck; they would commandeer the U.S. arsenal located on the Neck. Rolla Bennett would kill the governor and the mayor and then lead another attack through the city. His men would also stand guard to keep whites from nearby Cannonsborough from entering the city and quelling the rebellion. Gullah Jack's group was supposed to raid the gun shop and other stores and seize arms. Vesey himself would lead an attack from his house to the main guardhouse, where the men under his command would link forces with Poyas.

Vesey assumed that after the rebels had subdued Charleston, Haitians as well as other blacks would come to the city and help extend the revolution throughout the South. At the very least, he expected the slaves he was about to free to escape to Haiti.

On the afternoon of Saturday, June 15, the leaders of the revolt met at Vesey's house to put their months of preparation into action. A slave named Frank Ferguson who was also at the meeting told the revolt leaders that he had recently succeeded in convincing two slaves in St. John's Parish to lead an attack on Charleston. Vesey then asked one of his men, Jesse Blackwood, to inform the slaves in St. John's Parish that the date of the rebellion had been moved up. Blackwood was unable to spread the word, however. A military patrol refused to let him leave Charleston.

On Sunday, somewhere between 20 and 30 of
Vesey's rural supporters managed to reach the city by
canoe. They joined up with about 1,000 men who
were already in place in Charleston, waiting for the
attack to commence. But Vesey, who had begun to
suspect that the authorities knew of his plans, ordered
the revolutionaries to leave the city and await further
instructions. Meanwhile, he burned his list bearing
the names of the conspirators.

As soon as the attack was called off, all the carefully made plans began to unravel. On Monday, 10
members of the conspiracy were promptly arrested,
beginning with Peter Poyas and Ned and Rolla Bennett. But because Vesey had organized his followers
in such a way that an informant could identify only
a few participants, the number of arrests did not re-
flect the actual size of the attempted rebellion.

Only one of the leaders, Monday Gell, ever provided information to the authorities. Most of the recruits who were caught never talked during the court proceedings, which began on June 19, although the authorities tried to get information from them by keeping the prisoners in separate cells so that they could not arrange to falsely corroborate each other's stories. Only one complete list and one partial list bearing names of the conspirators were ever found.

Nevertheless, some of the lesser figures in the revolt led the authorities to believe that Denmark Vesey had been in charge of the conspiracy. On June 20, an official search for him began. Vesey was finally located three days later, in the home of one of his wives.

The Charleston authorities wound up arresting 131 people. Each of them was tried in a courtroom

A slave being tried in court for taking part in a revolt. At the trials of Vesey and his followers, legal procedures fell by the wayside as court officials attempted to deal with the insurrection as swiftly as possible and lessen the fear that continued to spread throughout the white community.

where the procedures reflected the degree of outrage in the community. Legal principles, including the usual requirements for evidence, fell by the wayside. Ironically, slave owners provided the only source of protection or justice for the accused because they had an interest in safeguarding their "property."

All told, the trials lasted five and a half weeks. The proceedings were closed to the public to prevent widespread panic and to make sure that no guilty persons were forewarned of the testimony being given against them. Local troops made sure that all blacks not connected with the trials stayed away from the jail.

The accused were tried in two groups: those who were said to have planned the conspiracy and those who simply followed along. People belonging to the latter group were deported. A death sentence awaited those who attended meetings, contributed money and other resources, or showed no remorse after their initial hearings.

The judges (there were as many as seven at a given hearing) decided that none of the conspirators would receive a sentence of capital punishment if convicted on the testimony of only one witness. Nor would they be put to death without any circumstantial evidence. Yet the judges did not need to reach a unanimous decision before sentencing a man to his death.

Ned Bennett, Rolla Bennett, Batteau Bennett, Peter Poyas, and Jesse Blackwood were among the first of the conspirators to be brought to trial. All were condemned to death.

Denmark Vesey was tried on June 23, with Colonel George Warren Cross serving as his counsel. William Paul was one of five witness who accused Vesey of heading the conspiracy. Vesey was allowed to cross-examine the men but failed to trap them into contradicting one another. Then he took one last tack:

He told the court it was ridiculous to think that a free black would lead a revolt. After all, what did he have to gain by such an action?

Vesey's remarks—as eloquent as they were—did not convince the judges, however. On June 28, the presiding official told the accused:

> Denmark Vesey—The Court, on mature consideration, have pronounced you Guilty—You have enjoyed the advantage of able Counsel, and were also heard in your own defence, in which you endeavored, with great art and plausibility, to impress a belief of your innocence. After the most patient deliberation, however, the Court were not only satisfied of your guilt, but that you were the author, and original instigator of this diabolical plot. Your professed design was to trample on all laws, human and divine; to riot in blood, outrage, . . . and conflagration, and to introduce anarchy and confusion in their most horrid forms. Your life has become, therefore, a just and necessary sacrifice, at the shrine of indignant Justice. It is difficult to imagine what *infatuation* could have prompted you to attempt an enterprise so wild and visionary. You were a free man; were comparatively wealthy; and enjoyed every comfort, compatible with your situation. You had, therefore, much to risk, and little to gain. From your age and experience you *ought* to have known, that success was impracticable.
>
> A moment's reflection must have convinced you, that the ruin of *your race*, would have been the probable result, and that years' would have rolled away, before they could have recovered that confidence, which, they once enjoyed in this community. The only reparation in your power, is a full disclosure of the truth. In addition to treason, you have committed the grossest impiety, in attempting to pervert the sacred words of God into a sanction for crimes of the blackest hue.

The following Tuesday, July 2, Vesey and five of his leaders were hanged on Blake's Lands, near Charleston. Their followers were so faithful that they planned to rescue their leaders on the day of execution. But the community was on alert, and more conspirators were arrested, including the last of Vesey's lieutenants, Gullah Jack. He was hanged 10 days later, on July 12.

Because most of the leaders were members of the Hampstead African Church, the authorities permanently closed down the church. Morris Brown, the founder, remained under suspicion, even though he was out of town on the day of the attempted revolt. He returned voluntarily for the trial and was questioned and released. Friends, fearing for his safety, helped him flee Charleston. Peter Prioleau, who had acted as an informant, was granted his freedom by the South Carolina legislature.

Of the 131 people who were arrested, 48 were whipped and released for lack of evidence, 26 were acquitted (but of these 11 were deported), and 67 were convicted for their part in the rebellion. Between June 18 and August 9, 35 of those convicted were put to death. Some of the bodies were left hanging for several days as a warning to other slaves and free blacks.

Yet Vesey's careful planning had protected many of the conspirators from the hangman's noose. The authorities never discovered the names of all those involved. None of the 600 recruits on Poyas's list were ever arrested or betrayed. Indeed, to this day, it is not known how many thousands of slaves were prepared to destroy Charleston on that summer night in 1822. Estimates have put the figure as high as 9,000.

One month after Vesey's execution, Governor Bennett published his account of the insurrection so the public could see how widespread the plot had been and how ably his officials had handled the matter. Later that month, another, longer version of the rebellion was published at the bidding of the city council. The public's overwhelming interest in this

AN

OFFICIAL REPORT

OF THE

TRIALS OF SUNDRY NEGROES,

CHARGED

with an Attempt to Raise

AN INSURRECTION

IN THE STATE OF SOUTH CAROLINA:

PRECEDED BY AN

INTRODUCTION AND NARRATIVE;

And in an Appendix,

A REPORT OF THE TRIALS OF

FOUR WHITE PERSONS,

ON INDICTMENTS FOR ATTEMPTING TO EXCITE THE SLAVES TO
INSURRECTION.

Prepared and Published at the request of the Court,
By Lionel H. Kennedy & Thomas Parker,
Members of the Charleston Bar, and the
Presiding Magistrates of the Court

CHARLESTON
Printed by James R. Schenck, 23 Broad Street

1822

The title page of the 48-page "official report" of Vesey's insurrection published by Charleston's city council in August 1822. This account became so popular that during the next few months four more editions of the pamphlet were printed.

48-page pamphlet prompted a 202-page account of the uprising to be published that November.

In the years immediately following Denmark Vesey's rebellion, South Carolina became even more alert to the possibility of insurrections. Slaves were no longer allowed to hire out, and a public assembly of any type was banned for slaves. Free blacks more than 15 years old had to have a white guardian. Blacks from Mexico, the Caribbean, and South America were not allowed to enter the state. Even black crews of ships in the Charleston harbor were forced to remain on board. The South could no longer pretend that slaves were content to labor for their owners.

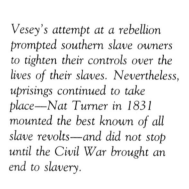

Vesey's attempt at a rebellion prompted southern slave owners to tighten their controls over the lives of their slaves. Nevertheless, uprisings continued to take place—Nat Turner in 1831 mounted the best known of all slave revolts—and did not stop until the Civil War brought an end to slavery.

The struggle against slavery did not end with the failure of revolts such as Vesey's. Instead, the fight went on. The voices of abolitionists grew louder and stronger. Blacks continued to believe that someday the nation would pay for slavery with bloodshed. And new fighters emerged to take over the battle when others fell victim to the hangman's noose.

In 1829, David Walker, a former slave who had escaped to Boston, Massachusetts, published a book, *David Walker's Appeal to the Colored Citizens of the*

World, But in Particular, and Very Expressly, to Those of The United States of America, that called on all Americans to overthrow the system of slavery, even if it meant using force to do so. "Had you not rather be killed than be a slave to a tyrant?" he asked his audience. That same year, several slave revolts took place in Louisiana.

Then, on August 21, 1831, in South Hampton County, Virginia, Nat Turner led what has become the best-known of all slave rebellions. By the time the Virginia militia had put down his revolt, 60 whites and more than 100 blacks lay dead. Turner was captured on October 30 and executed on November 11. Nevertheless, his revolt, like Vesey's, terrified the South. Turner's rebellion had made it clear that the positive-good theory was nothing but a lie and that any slave might turn out to be the leader of a revolt.

Indeed, throughout the history of slavery in the United States, slaves always resisted their oppression, and their resistence took on many forms. Some tried to protect themselves and their families by pretending to be obedient. Others resisted by stealing from their owners or by destroying property. A fair number of slaves managed to run away, finding freedom in the northern states or in Canada. And a few, like Vesey and Turner—and Gabriel Prosser before them—decided to change the system by force, no matter what the cost.

These men were living proof that wherever people are enslaved, there will be those who demand fair treatment and fight against oppression, even if it means using violence. The slave system in America, after all, was a violent system of oppression. And it took a long and bloody civil war to end it. ✧

CHRONOLOGY

——— ❦ ———

1767	Denmark Vesey is born (in either the Caribbean or Africa)
1781	Is sold into slavery on St. Domingue; becomes Captain Joseph Vesey's personal slave and works on slave-trading vessels
1783	Moves with Joseph Vesey to Charleston, South Carolina, and begins hiring himself out as a carpenter
1799	Wins $1,500 in the Bay Street Lottery
1800	Purchases his freedom from Joseph Vesey for $600 and buys a home near Charleston
1817	Becomes a member of the Hampstead Methodist Church
1821	Makes plans for a slave revolt; begins recruiting slaves and free blacks
May 31, 1822	Several of Denmark Vesey's men are arrested and interrogated by the Charleston city council
June 8, 1822	Denmark Vesey changes the date of the revolt from July 14 to June 16
June 16, 1822	Cancels the slave rebellion
June 20, 1822	City officials launch a search for Denmark Vesey
June 23, 1822	Denmark Vesey is captured and brought to trial
June 28, 1822	City officials find Denmark Vesey guilty of raising an insurrection
July 2, 1822	Denmark Vesey is hanged on Blake's Lands, near Charleston

FURTHER READING

Aptheker, Herbert. *American Negro Slave Revolts*. New York: International Publishers, 1952.

Berlin, Ira. *Slaves Without Masters: The Free Negro in the Antebellum South*. New York: Vintage, 1974.

Franklin, John Hope, and Alfred A. Moss, Jr. *From Slavery to Freedom: A History of Negro Americans*. 6th ed. New York: Knopf, 1988.

Goldin, Claudia Dale. *Urban Slavery in the American South, 1820–1860: A Quantitative History*. Chicago: University of Chicago Press, 1976.

Higginbotham, A. Leon, Jr. *In the Matter of Color—Race & the American Legal Process: The Colonial Period*. New York: Oxford University Press, 1978.

Jordan, Winthrop. *White over Black: American Attitudes Toward the Negro, 1550–1812*. New York: Norton, 1977.

Kennedy, Lionel H., and Thomas Parker. *The Trial Record of Denmark Vesey*. Boston: Beacon Press, 1970.

Lofton, John. *Denmark Vesey's Revolt: The Slave Plot That Lit a Fuse to Fort Sumter*. Kent, OH: Kent State University Press, 1983.

———. *Insurrection in South Carolina: The Turbulent World of Denmark Vesey*. Yellow Springs, OH: Antioch Press, 1964.

Wade, Richard. *Slavery in the Cities: The South, 1820–1860*. London: Oxford Unversity Press, 1964.

INDEX

PICTURE CREDITS

LILLIE J. EDWARDS is associate professor of history at DePaul University, where she teaches in the undergraduate honors program and the masters in liberal arts program at the College of Arts and Sciences. She has also taught at the University of North Carolina at Chapel Hill and at Earlham College, where she was director of the African and African-American studies program and faculty leader of the 1982 foreign studies program in Kenya. She holds a B.A. degree in history and English from Oberlin College and a Ph.D. in African history, with concentrations in U.S. southern history and African literature, from the University of Chicago.

A member of the Organization of American Historians and the American Historical Association, Dr. Edwards has served on the program committee for the Association of Afro-American Life and History and the nominations committee for the Association of Black Women Historians. She has also served as a consultant and program reviewer for the Humanities Division of the New Jersey State Board of Education, the Exxon Educational Foundation, and the National Endowment of the Humanities. Among her awards are the W. E. B. Du Bois doctoral fellowship at Harvard University and the Rockefeller Grant for Minority-Group Scholars.

Her published works include *Black American Missionaries in Colonial Africa—Materials About Black Americans* (1981); "Black Americans in British and Portuguese colonies," in Sylvia Jacob's *Black American Missionaries* (1982); and several articles in the *Dictionary of American Christianity* (1989). She is currently writing a book about Afro-American missionaries and editing a book of essays on Afro-American religion.

NATHAN IRVIN HUGGINS is W.E.B. Du Bois Professor of History and Director of the W.E.B. Du Bois Institute for Afro-American Research at Harvard University. He previously taught at Columbia University. Professor Huggins is the author of numerous books, including *Black Odyssey: The Afro-American Ordeal in Slavery*, *The Harlem Renaissance*, and *Slave and Citizen: The Life of Frederick Douglass*.